HOLES

Cosmic Gushers in the Universe

JOHN GRIBBIN

A DELTA BOOK

A DELTA BOOK

Published by
Dell Publishing Co., Inc.
1 Dag Hammarskjold Plaza
New York, New York 10017

Originally published in Great Britain by Paladin Books

Published by arrangement with Delacorte Press/Eleanor Friede

Delta ® TM   755118, Dell Publishing Co., Inc.

ISBN: 0-440-59521-5

Printed in the United States of America
Second Delta printing—April 1978

VB

To Bill McCrea

My first (and best) guide to matters cosmological

Science is far more exciting than science fiction,
far more intricate, far more subtle—
and science has the additional virtue of being true.

Carl Sagan

The more I see, the more I see there is to see.

John Sebastian

CONTENTS

vii

Contents

INTRODUCTION:
Astronomical Tigers and Sheep

Things are not as they seem in the jungle of our Universe. There, where every shadow contains some mysterious tiger (not always burning bright), astronomers must struggle with the inadequacy of their senses, supported by the props of electronic equipment, to fathom just what immortal hand or eye *did* shape the cosmos.

To most people (and to many astronomers still) the Universe seems to be a glorious puzzle of more or less constant phenomena that can be observed in turn until sufficient pieces are gathered and the overall picture emerges. The stars and galaxies, for example, are simply *there,* waiting to be observed, changing little in the human world view. But this simple approach is rapidly becoming out of date. The first indications from relativity theory that everything is connected to everything else—that the overall structure of the Universe is as important as the details—have now evolved into paradigms for a new world view. But within this new framework the problems of explaining simple observations loom almost as large as before.

Philosophers have long argued the question of how far

man can trust his senses. A tale is told of two men walking in the countryside who observe some sheep grazing on a distant hill. "Ah," says the first, "I see those sheep have been sheared recently." The other, more cautious, replies, "It certainly seems so, from this side." Real life experience tells us that if sheep are shorn on one side they surely are shorn on the other—but can we be equally certain about objects we see in the depths of space?

Insights which have led to the greatest advances in the development of our world view have come from those thinkers able to make the great leap of asking how things would be if they were not as they seem to our senses, which have been conditioned by everyday life; able to ask: what if the sheep are not shorn on the other side? This method of progress has continued from the time that man first puzzled about the Universe in the dim reaches of prehistory, through the earliest documentation that has come down to us, until now. The fundamental urge to seek abstract knowledge about how and why we are here is a basic factor distinguishing human beings from other animals. Even dolphins with their theoretical potential to be humans' intellectual equals (some would say they are potentially superior) devote their considerable brain power to the control of their immediate environment, the sea, to which they are superbly adapted, and they seem not to have been beset by the urge to know how their local environment fits into the greater

environment of the total Universe—the urge that has been the driving force behind many of the most significant intellectual achievements of the human race. This fundamental human urge remains, whatever it is called, whether religion, philosophy, astrology, astronomy, or cosmology. Under its variety of semantic guises over the centuries, this desire to know has brought such progress that today we have a knowledge of the Universe that encompasses a range hardly dreamed of by our ancestors.

This is not to say that there is an end to the search—we still have no evidence of any single answer to the question posed by our existence. Indeed, the more we know, the more it becomes clear how much remains to be understood. The growth of knowledge might be likened to an expanding balloon, with the volume of air inside the balloon representing the known and the skin of the balloon marking the boundary between the known and the unknown. As the volume of the known increases, so does the surface area of the balloon—the extent of the boundary between the known and the unknown—so that the more we see, the more we see there is to see. Life is more complicated for us than it was for the ancients who were able to accept most events in their lives as the will of a god or the gods. Our increased understanding of the Universe has not been a smooth, steady progression over the centuries. Throughout history, new insights into the nature of the Universe and man's place in it have appeared as great imaginative or intuitive leaps, sometimes made by a single thinker but often by several people in a similar form at roughly the same time. These imaginative leaps have then been followed by a period of consolidation in which the dramatic new insight has been woven into the fabric of the general consciousness until it has become a commonplace. Who, now, doubts the Earth is round? But this was once an heretical thought. Then, when the time is again right, another great leap forward reveals a new perspective to be incorporated into man's ever evolving understanding of the Universe.

Take the example of the shape of the Earth. Once, the philosopher might have pondered the nature of the edge of the flat Earth or how it was supported from underneath, but he would not have wondered if the Earth were round—not, that is, without giving up the accepted world view of his time. It takes a great deal of imagination to go beyond the accepted, to question, to ask: what if . . . ? What, for example, if the Earth were not flat, the Sun not the center of the Universe, the stars not lights fixed to the crystal spheres? Of course, the kind of imagination that is not bound by the ordinary conventions sometimes comes up with ideas that turn out to be wrong, and these fail to become part of a new cosmic view. As great imaginers are not always the best practical testers of their own ideas, it is only *after* the initial creative leap of imagination that the scientific method of testing hypotheses comes into its own. The idea of a round Earth must have been laughed to scorn many times before the implications were considered seriously by the scientific community of the day. Only then, with a change in thinking, could it have been seen that if the Earth were round then the hill formed by the curvature would obscure the hull of a distant ship even when its masts became visible; that a round Earth would explain why a lookout high on a ship's mast can see farther than from the deck; why we cannot see right to the edge even on the clearest day—there seemed to be something in this crazy idea after all!

A New World Picture

Only after the idea of a round Earth had become part of generally accepted thinking could a new imaginative leap be made from the secure foundation of a now *improved* world view. Many people are involved in filling in the details of each new world view, but very few have the imagination to provide the skeleton to be filled in. The last major imaginative leap forward came more than a half century ago with the formulation of the ideas of relativity and quantum theory, and only now, after more than fifty years of filling in, has a clear new world picture emerged—and it is still too early to say that it has become the commonsense view. Is it simple common sense that the faster an object moves, the more its mass increases and the slower it ages? Is it literally impossible to say precisely just where a small particle is *and* where it is going?

If your answer to those questions is no, then I hope that you may change your opinions after reading this book, because these are far from being the most bizarre implications of the new view of the nature of the cosmos. Along the way, you may have to revise your ideas about many familiar concepts such as mass, time, and weight. Take weight: we all know that weight is an intrinsic property of any object, don't we? Actually, however, that is not so. It is the mass of the body that is its intrinsic property and by which the amount of material in the object is measured, essentially in terms of the number and kind of atoms of which the object is comprised. The weight of the object is the force which results from the interaction of that mass with the mass of the whole Earth —an interaction we call gravity, though we do not fully understand it. If, for example, a kilo of weight were moved to the Moon, it would contain the same mass as on the Earth, but its weight, measured on a spring balance, would be only one-sixth of a kilo, because the Moon is smaller than the Earth and contains less mass than the Earth. Similarly, as the Skylab flight showed, in free-fall the weight of everything is zero—astronauts, tools, food, everything can float without falling at all, relative to each other.

In the space programs of the U.S. and the USSR, we see science fiction becoming science fact. These programs are providing one of the biggest boosts ever for revising the common view of the Universe more into line with recent imaginative leaps.[1] The imagination of the science-fiction writers has been, in many cases, simply a reworking of the imagination of great scientists of the past and present. This is not to belittle science fiction. Because the imaginative leaps of a great thinker such as Einstein or Newton are beyond the grasp of the commonsense mind, the science-fiction writer fulfills a vital role in popularizing new ideas and easing them into the world view of ordinary people. Science fiction must be based on the same kind of imaginative speculation as the great science-fact developments, but it will always have to fall short of the best science-fact imagination. I shall return often to this theme, as it seems to me more than mere coincidence that the development of science fiction to its present height has occurred during the half century it has so far taken to assimilate into the popular consciousness some

7

of the greatest imaginative leaps science has ever produced. These ideas have become the practical reality of engineering plans and constructions only after passing through the filter of science fiction, and there is much more on its way through that same filter.

An example may clarify the distinction between the type of imagination possessed by the creative scientist and the science-fiction writer and that underlying the skills of the applications engineer. One of the most common devices used in scientific and engineering mathematics is the quadratic equation or its equivalent. This equation involves the square of an unknown quantity. In solving such equations, there are always two possible solutions corresponding to the fact that any square can be arrived at in two ways [for example, *16* may be obtained either as *4 × 4* or as *(−4) × (−4)*]. Though these two solutions are not usually merely the same numbers with plus or minus signs in front of them, that is the simplest example. To an engineer—perhaps one designing a Moon rocket—the solution to a particular problem will usually seem obvious. If he finds that the negative root corresponds to a Moon rocket that begins its journey by burrowing into the ground, that can obviously be discarded as a bad world view. However, an imaginative scientist faced with the same set of equations might ask: what if . . . ? What if a Moon rocket did first burrow into the ground? Ridiculous? Certainly—but no more so than the concept of tachyons.

There are also two sorts of solutions to the quadratic equations of relativity theory. One corresponds to particles which always travel slower than the speed of light —a piece of Einsteinian theory now almost completely accepted—while the other corresponds to particles which always travel faster than light. The imagination needed to accept that the reality of both solutions goes beyond Einstein's world view; the concept of tachyons—those faster-than-light particles—has not yet gained general acceptance. It is discussed today only in a handful of advanced scientific papers and, increasingly, in the literature of science fiction. How long will it take, I wonder, before this new imaginative leap is used by sober engineers to design communicators with which we can transmit and receive messages that traverse the Galaxy faster than the speed of light?

Imagination—backed up by practical tests to determine which imaginative leaps are securely founded—is the key to a more accurate world picture. This book is an outline of the most up-to-date view of the Universe resulting from the latest series of imaginative leaps made by the creative thinkers that today we call scientists—rather than prophets, seers, or oracles—for, when it comes to gaining fundamental new insights, the words mean the same.

One of the latest imaginative advances has already received, more or less as an isolated topic, so much popular attention that it is on the verge of becoming common knowledge, even though the basis for it remains well into the realm of pure imaginative science. I refer to the concept of black holes as a kind of ultimate sink, or plughole in the Universe, which drains matter away.

The saga of the black holes has caught the popular imagination more than any other aspect of the new astronomy—and it is easy to see why. These ultimate sinks had been predicted by relativists in the second quarter of the present century. As relativity theory is now respectable, black holes are clothed with respectability.

Bizarre though they may seem in everyday terms, an astronomer brought up in the old school can, though perhaps with a bit of discomfort, stretch his mind to accommodate the concept, and in those terms black holes are the most bizarre of phenomena imaginable, the ultimate oddity of the old astronomy. But, of course, the old astronomy is not the complete world picture, and stretching it to accommodate black holes is simply not enough. These objects may be the most peculiar features of the old astronomy, but they are among the simplest and most obvious features of the new astronomy. Once the idea of black holes gets into the world view, the rest of the new astronomy inexorably follows, almost as if the new ideas get in through the holes.

In the old picture, these holes in space are the ultimate end-point of matter—everything eventually collapses down into such a state that the intense gravity prevents anything, even light, from escaping. And that is the end of the matter. But, in the new astronomy, these holes are seen as a beginning. If things can go into black holes, then, by reversing a sign in the equation (what if . . . ?), we find that things can come out from—let's call them *white holes*. And with a little more imagination, the equations can be interpreted to suggest links between black and white holes, tunnels forming a cosmic subway, so that in a real sense what goes in must come out.

This is not idle speculation. The greatest enigma of the old astronomy, never successfully resolved, was the intensely energetic sources of the Universe where matter seems to be pouring out from a tiny central region. At a stroke, the new astronomy resolves this problem while retaining conventional nuclear physics which

explains why the Sun and the stars stay hot and bright
for so long.

To mix the metaphor, the black hole is merely the
tip of the iceberg of the new astronomy; and the new
world view is as great an advance, and as shattering a
revolution in thought, as the concept of a round Earth
orbiting the Sun was in its day. Furthermore, with
hindsight, the new world view is as simple to understand
as other once revolutionary ideas. There is little that is
new in this book—in the sense that the ideas here have
long been discussed by the philosophers, relativists, and
mathematicians who today continue the traditions of
Galileo, Newton, and Einstein. However, outside the
scientific elite circle, even science-fiction readers are not
yet acquainted with the full, breathtaking vista of the
new world picture. The professionals may find what
follows to be familiar and dull, but, in the words of the
pulps, new readers begin here.

PROLOGUE 1:
Black Holes: A Figment
of the Imagination?

There is nothing new about the idea of black holes. As long ago as 1798 the great French mathematician and astronomer, Pierre Simon de Laplace (1749–1827), realized that even in the context of the straightforward Newtonian theory of gravity, stars might exist from which no light could escape, that they subsequently would appear as black holes in space. The argument is very simple. Because of the pull of gravity, anything traveling more slowly than the escape velocity will either fall back to the parent body or enter a closed orbit around it as an artificial satellite. Now, this critical escape velocity increases either if the mass of the parent body is increased or if the radius of the parent body is decreased. We will look at the second possibility later. What Laplace postulated was that the escape velocity from it would increase indefinitely if more mass could be added to a body in space, increasing its radius but not its density. For example, a star with the same density as our Sun but with a radius as large as the orbit of the Earth around the Sun would have an escape velocity greater than the speed of light—an incredible 300,000 kilometers a second. The gravity from such a star would cause rays of light to be bent back towards their origin on the surface of the star and photons (light particles) could orbit around the star in the same manner that the Moon orbits the Earth. However, no special significance was attached to Laplace's theory for many years because there was no reason to imagine that a star with the same density as our Sun, but stretching across the equivalent of the Earth's orbit, could exist, and, even if it did, we would be unable to detect it because of this very black-hole effect. It was not until 1917, when astronomers and mathematicians were struggling to come to terms (as they still are) with all the implications of Einstein's general theory of relativity, which has revolutionized our thinking about gravity during this century, that the idea of black holes appeared again, in a rather different guise.

Even in the late thirties, when mathematicians began to produce detailed equations describing the properties of black holes, it seemed that these objects would surely remain just part of the scientific imagination. How, after all, could observers expect to detect an object which, according to the equations, did not radiate anything? The philosophical basis for the study of black holes seemed akin to an earlier debate about the number of angels that could dance on the head of a pin; if your best theory of the Universe posits that something exists, but that this something is invisible and undetectable, can it then be claimed that the object really exists, in the general understanding of that term?

Therefore, black holes might be a figment of the imagination—or, rather, a figment of the mathematics used to describe the Universe, mathematics which might not be entirely correct. Perhaps a better theory could

NGC 6205. Globular star cluster in Hercules. Messier 13.
Enl : 1.7 x 200-in. Hale.
Photograph from the Hale Observatories

supersede Einstein's if it removed the mathematical foundation of the concept of black holes by correcting an imperfection in the general theory of relativity? It seemed to be an esoteric argument of no practical value, one which could never be resolved by direct observation. But less than ten years ago astronomers working with new instruments to observe new features of the Universe discovered sources of energy within our Galaxy of unprecedented intensity: bright X-ray stars and pulsars. The mathematicians were quick to realize that such intense energy was associated with strong gravitational fields and that these offered an opportunity to test the predictions of the general theory of relativity. It was possible that a black hole might be detected—if not directly then by its influence on nearby material.

The Dynamics of Gravity

Though we don't totally understand gravity, we do know quite a bit about how things behave when gravity tugs at them. A falling object, tugged by gravity, quickly picks up the energy of motion, which it gains from the gravitational interaction. Drop a bottle a few inches from the ground, and it will probably settle with no damage done because it wouldn't have picked up enough energy from the motion to rearrange its molecular structure. Drop the same bottle from a great height, and

it will be thoroughly rearranged when the energy it has picked up falling through the gravity of the Earth is redistributed in new ways on impact. This rearrangement shows that the energy of motion is shared out among the different bits of infalling material—ultimately among the individual atoms of the falling material—whenever anything under the pull of gravity is involved in collision. At the level of atomic particles, energy of motion is exactly equivalent to heat energy. Energy picked up in this way is radiated away as heat or light the same way a hot iron bar will radiate away its energy as visible light, which we can see, and as heat, which we can feel. The more energy put in, the more comes out as radiation; therefore, it is clear that sources of very strong radiation in the Universe are getting energy from somewhere. One of the best ways to derive energy from a compact source is to drop matter onto it, letting gravity do the work. And the more compact the underlying object, the more the material hitting it is knocked about during collision, and the more energy is radiated away. The compact kind of black hole provides both a very strong gravitational pull and a very small target area for infalling matter.

So, in the seventies, the discovery of compact high-energy sources so hot they radiated X-rays again brought forth the study of black holes, though the idea was already at least one and a half centuries old and had been studied for thirty years as an abstract example of the mathematical arts within the framework of the general theory of relativity. However, revival of interest in black holes has come about through investigations opposite to the approach of Laplace. Instead of adding mass to constant density, thus swelling out the size of a star, a black hole can arise through the compression of an existing mass—whether it be a star, a planet, or a teaspoon—to a high enough density. Because the escape velocity depends on mass, it is much easier for a big mass to compress to the critical limit, and a big mass has the further characteristic that its own gravity will already be strongly pulling all the material in the body toward the center.

Gravitational attraction of the material depends on the mass of the body; it takes the pull of the mass of the entire Earth to keep us from floating off into space. Since it takes a whole planet to pull *me* down with a weight of less than 200 pounds, gravity seems a pretty feeble force. A small object easily can resist the feeble gravity of its own small mass, and the Earth can comfortably hold itself up against gravity by the resistance of the crystal structures of rocks to compression, and, indeed, by the resistance of atoms themselves. This weak gravity force has, however, two properties that make it a force to be reckoned with in the Universe in general. First, it is a very long-range force; although it dies away as the square of the distance from any mass, the Sun, for example, keeps a gravitational grip on tiny Pluto as that planet circles at the fringe of the Solar System forty times farther from the Sun than the Earth is. The whole Solar System is kept orbiting around our Galaxy of stars by the determined tug of gravity acting over distances of tens of thousands of times greater still. Thus, the farther out you look, the more significant gravity becomes. This is partly because of the second major attribute of gravity: the way the pull of a body increases as its mass increases. With objects as massive as stars, holding material up against the continuing persistent tug of gravity becomes a real problem.

How Stars Die

While a star is young, it is hot, and the problem does not arise. Gravity, in fact, first creates a star like our Sun. A cloud of gas in space collapses under gravity, forming a roughly spherical mass which then heats up as the potential energy of the gas is converted to kinetic and heat energy during the shrinking process. When the center is hot enough, nuclear reactions begin. These fuse atomic nuclei and release still more energy, which makes the star shine and provides the force of pressure that stops the center from collapsing further. This nuclear fusion can only continue until all the light elements have been fused, or burnt, leaving the stellar equivalent of ash—heavy elements such as iron from which no more energy can be extracted by fusion. This takes thousands of millions of year. All that time gravity has been waiting patiently, never weakening, until the resistance to further collapse is halted. And, once a star is burnt out, collapse can continue into one of three possible states.

If the dying star has about the same mass—that is, the same quantity of material—as our Sun (strictly, no more than 1.2 times the mass of the Sun), then it can become a dwarf, a dead star in which the fusion products such as iron settle into a cold crystal lattice the strength of which holds the star up against its own gravity. While the dead star is settling into this state, but is still hot and bright, it is called a white dwarf; as it cools it eventually will become a red dwarf and then a black dwarf, basically a cold lump of iron and other elements, as massive as our Sun but no bigger than the Earth.

Stars containing more than 1.2 times as much material as our Sun, but less than three solar masses of matter, have an inward pull of gravity able to crush atoms out of existence, producing a denser, more stable state. Negatively charged electrons and positively charged protons, the atomic building blocks, are squeezed together until most of the star's matter is converted into neutral (uncharged) neutrons. The whole star becomes one giant droplet of neutrons—the size of a large mountain —containing twice as much matter as the Sun. This is the ultimate compact state of matter as we know it: a whole star as dense as the nucleus of an atom. It might follow that the neutron star state represents the ultimate immovable object against which the irresistible force of gravity must be spent—surely nothing can crush neutrons?

In fact, the immovable object is not immovable at all and the irresistible force really is irresistible. According to the best available theories, a strong enough gravitational field can crush even neutrons and can squeeze matter into a mathematical point. The strength of the field necessary for such a remarkable occurrence would be produced by a star more massive than two or three suns (theories differ on the exact critical mass that would be required) as it collapses to, and beyond, the neutron star state after its fusion fuel is spent.

Obviously, such a collapse towards a point—a mathematical singularity—cannot be observed from outside; before the collapse goes that far, the density will have become so great that the escape velocity exceeds the speed of light, making the collapsing star disappear into a black hole. This is even more frustrating than the Laplacian version of black holes. Now, so the mathematics tell us, matter literally can be squeezed out of existence, with some very curious side effects, but only in places where it is impossible to see what is going on. Black holes in themselves are not at all exciting—the mysterious and fantastic stories we have heard about them in recent years really depend on these mathematical singularities. The singularities are exciting but they are hidden inside the black holes. Where is the edge of the black hole?

In 1917 Schwarzschild determined, from the theory of relativity, the boundary where the escape velocity reaches the speed of light. It is called the Schwarzschild radius. In round numbers, the Schwarzschild radius for any object is given in kilometers by dividing the mass of the object by the mass of the Sun and multiplying by three. And that is the radius within which an object must be compressed, or collapsed, before it will become a black hole. As the mass of the Sun is 2×10^{30} kilograms (that is, 2 followed by 30 zeros), it is easy to see how small the Schwarzschild radius is for an everyday object such as a teaspoon.

Time Perspectives

Even if we could watch through telescopes the collapse of a star three times as massive as our Sun, we would not be able to see anything happening once the star had shrunk within its own Schwarzschild radius. Moreover, it is not merely a matter of watching the star collapse like a punctured balloon and wink out as it reaches the critical radius, because time itself is affected by gravitational fields strong enough to trap light. Exactly what seems to happen to the collapsing star will depend on from where the observations are made and, in particular, the situation would seem very different to two observers if one were sitting on the surface of the star and one were safely outside. The *relative* positions of the two observers are important.

To the outside observer, it would seem that the star collapsed more and more slowly as it neared the Schwarzschild radius, with the collapse taking infinite time on the clocks outside the embryonic black hole. Once the star approached the limiting radius, a collapse that slow would be undetectable and the star would seem unchanging—indeed some early investigators of the theory of black holes used the term frozen stars to describe them. Actually, we would not be able to see the frozen star forever from our imagined grandstand seat outside, even with the aid of the most powerful telescopes, because the star fades from view within a few hundred-thousandths of a second.

This seems like a contradiction—the collapse seems to take forever, yet the star disappears quicker than the blink of an eye—but there is a simple explanation. Light is still leaving the region outside the Schwarzschild radius, but almost all its energy is expended climbing away from the gravitational pull of the collapsing star. This is the opposite of the way anything falling under the pull of gravity gains energy. In getting out uphill against the pull of gravity, anything—from a rocketship to the electromagnetic radiation we know as light—will lose energy. Getting out of a deep hole is hard work, and the light gets tired. For a rocket, losing energy would mean going

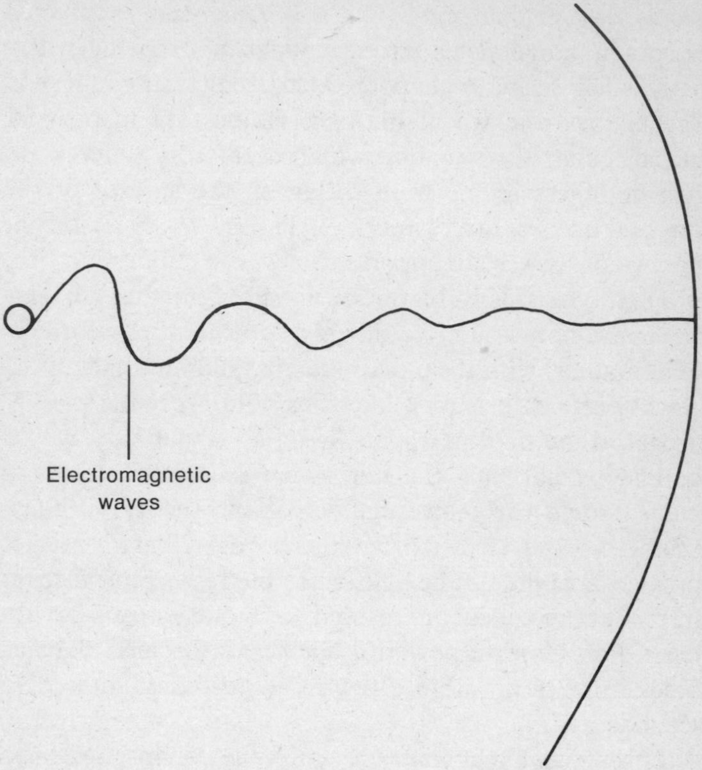

Electromagnetic
waves

Schwarzschild
radius

Figure 1

As it sets off, radiation trying to get out of a black hole waves vigorously, producing a strong signal visible to anyone around near the singularity to see it. But climbing up out of the hole weakens the signal, which is stretched by the strong gravity. The waves get smaller and smaller until at the Schwarzschild radius they have disappeared—the electromagnetic signal of the light waves has been stretched out of existence, and no one outside the hole will see anything.

22

slower but as the speed of light is always constant (300 thousand kilometers a second), for light to lose energy in this way (the gravitational red shift) simply means that the wave length of the light increases and the signal contained in the wave becomes too faint to be detected. This red shift effect is one of the best ways of understanding how a black hole can trap light completely. Once the collapsing object reaches its Schwarzschild radius, the gravitational red shift becomes infinite—that is, the electromagnetic waves of a light signal are stretched out of existence altogether and there is no signal left for outside observers to detect.

But what about the observer on the surface of the collapsing star? To him, or to anyone rash enough to chase after a shrinking star in a spaceship, the Schwarzschild radius, which is so important for light signals, is crossed with no difficulty—it is not a physical barrier like a solid wall or even like the sound barrier for aircraft. The observer would only know he was inside a black hole if he made careful measurements, or if he tried to get out, which would, of course, be impossible. And he would not notice anything peculiar happening to his own clocks even though his time would seem almost infinitely slowed to outside observers as he approached the Schwarzschild radius.

The development of the *outside* Universe would seem to him to be greatly *speeded up* as he fell into the black hole, and he could continue to watch this with his own telescope since there is nothing to stop light going inward from crossing the Schwarzschild radius.

This difference in time rates has some uncomfortable features, but it also offers a genuine possibility of time travel, if only in one direction. A few years ago, after attention became focused on black holes, some of the better science-fiction writers incorporated the implications of them into their stories of the future. One disturbing little tale concerns two beings in telepathic contact with one another as they explore the region near a black hole in space. One of them falls through the Schwarzschild radius and into the singularity, being crushed out of existence in a few seconds of his own time. But the fall takes forever on the time-scale of his telepathic partner who must spend the rest of his life "listening" to the infinitely drawn out "telepathic scream of fear" emitted by his doomed companion. Of course, this tale does rather depend on how strong gravitational fields would affect telepathic waves. If such exist, it's probable that they, too, would be red shifted, fading out in a few thousandths of a second so that, although they might still be there in principle, they in fact would be undetectable. Perhaps we need not concern ourselves too much for the future telepathic explorers of space. There is, however, a completely genuine black-hole effect that would make a good basis for a science-fiction story.

This effect depends on the way time is slowed for the infalling observer, so that to him the outside Universe evolves more rapidly. The time dilation occurs not just inside the black hole but also in the region of strong gravity immediately outside the Schwarzschild radius. By judicious steering, an intrepid astronaut could dive close to this region on a parabolic orbit and swing up again into normal space afterward. Assuming he could find a black hole, this maneuver would not even require much power as the gravity of the black hole would do most of the work. During his close approach, his time rate would be slowed—he would seem to an outside observer to be almost in suspended animation—and when he emerged from the field he would find that time in the outside Universe had gone much more quickly than it had in his spaceship. This would be a way of moving rapidly forward in time, of traveling into the future. Just how far one could travel would depend on the size of the black hole and how closely one dared approach it, but one could make repeated flights, jumping across the centuries each time. The only snag, of course, would be that if you decided the future was unattractive you could not return.

Evidence of Black Holes

How likely is it that black holes really exist? At present, about 10 percent of the material that forms new stars in the Milky Way seems to go into stars more than ten times as massive as the Sun. This gives a "guesstimate" that there may be a thousand million black holes in our Galaxy, formed from previous generations of massive stars, and some astronomers argue that massive stars were even more numerous when our Galaxy was younger, so that there could be even more black holes to mark their graves. But could we ever detect such an object? Due to the very strong gravitational field of a black hole, the answer seems to be yes.

There would be very little prospect of discovering a black hole sitting quietly on its own in space. A black hole in the act of forming might produce a burst of gravitational radiation, but no one has yet been able to provide satisfactory evidence that this radiation could be detected with present-day equipment. Yet a sociable black hole, one orbiting in a binary embrace with a more normal companion star, would produce great floods of electromagnetic radiation because of its interaction with material tugged off its partner by tidal effects. This is just the sort of thing we now see in some celestial X-ray sources. Although very many of these objects can be explained by the presence of white dwarf or neutron stars, the consensus among astronomers today is that a few can be accounted for only by the presence of something more extreme—and that, as we know, means a black hole.

Material captured from the companion star forms a disc around the black hole, spiraling inward under the influence of its gravity and funneling through the throat of the Schwarzschild radius. That throat is not very large; a black hole that has developed from a collapsing star of three solar masses has a critical radius of only about ten kilometers. So, as the material falls inward, gaining kinetic energy and heating up as it loses gravitational potential energy, a turbulent whirlpool of colliding particles is produced. As there is no way the quantity of available material can slip through the throat, the result is a cloud of swirling material that is hot enough to radiate strongly at X-ray wave lengths. There are different theories about the amount of energy that can be liberated when matter falls into a black hole in this way. The ultimate would be for the entire mass to be converted into energy, in line with Einstein's $E = mc^2$, but this effect cannot be approached in practice. However, the amount of material converted into radiation will be at least 6 percent of this Einsteinian limit and perhaps 40 percent. That means that the black-hole process is at least ten times as effective at producing energy as the nuclear fusion that keeps the Sun hot and maybe sixty times more effective than the generation of stellar energy. Most of the energy in the cloud of hot material is liberated within a few Schwarzschild radii of the center, a region about a hundred kilometers across in the case of a hole of a few solar masses. The intense energy production of such a cloud produces erratic flickering of the source as material swirls around, as can be seen in some X-ray sources. This rapid flickering, evidence of extreme compactness, is the keystone of the belief that a couple of black holes orbiting more normal companion stars have been found. By 1980, when X-ray satellites are in orbit carrying telescopes ten thousand times more powerful than those available today, it should be possible to identify many such X-ray sources and to study their properties in detail. But, remember, even then astronomers will only be studying radiation from material *near* black holes. It is impossible to look inside the event horizon from outside; it is impossible to see the singularity at the heart of a black hole of this kind without taking the irrevocable step of crossing the event horizon into the black hole proper. As Martin Rees, Plumian Professor of Astronomy and Experimental Philosophy at the University of Cambridge, has put it, "One's Faustian urge must be sufficiently strong to venture inside the horizon despite the inevitable destruction this implies."

The Potentials of Black Holes

The above statement is true of the kind of black hole described so far, the kind that may have been found among the stars of the Milky Way—but there are other, even more curious possibilities, including the idea that we may ourselves be living in a black hole which contains our entire Universe. Thus, the words of Professor Rees do not limit the study of black holes and singularities as much as they might seem to at first consideration. Because of the dependence of the black-hole effect on mass as well as on density, very large black holes may live at the centers of galaxies, gobbling up whole stars without first disrupting them. There is certainly plenty of evidence that the nuclei of galaxies are regions of sometimes violent activity (up to and including outbursts on the scale of quasars), and this might well be a result of the presence of singularities, though these need not be black holes. Such activity is, in many ways, just the opposite of the kind of collapse that occurs with black holes, and galactic nuclei are perhaps the best sites to investigate for the presence of *white* holes— cosmic gushers exploding *outward* into the Universe. It has been argued at the other end of the scale that tiny black holes may have been created by the processes (whatever those were) that created the Universe. A hole the size of a proton, for example, would contain "only" a thousand million tons and could grow only by swallowing one proton or neutron at a time. Very many such objects *might* exist, and, dubious though it may sound, on the basis of observations of the dynamics of the Milky Way system, there is no reason why as much as half the mass seen in bright stars could not be present in our Galaxy as mini black holes. If such a hole acquired an electric charge (perhaps by swallowing more electrons than protons), we could even capture it and keep it safely suspended by electrical forces.

Prologue 1: Black Holes: A Figment of the Imagination?

The real importance of the possibility that mini black holes exist, however, is as a reminder that the Universe must be considered as a whole when we are investigating the fundamental peculiarities of space-time. By peering too closely at the details of a black hole made from the collapse of a star we could miss, as many have done, the grandeur of the broad sweep of space-time and the larger scale implications of the same equations that describe a black hole. The fact that black holes have been discovered as X-ray stars gives us a great deal of confidence in the accuracy of these equations. So, when we turn our attention to the whole Universe and our place in it, we can have more faith in the accuracy of our mathematical description than earlier astronomers. Before drawing back to look at the whole, however, it is worth pausing a little longer to study the not-quite-black holes of white dwarf and neutron stars.

PROLOGUE 2:
Before the Black Hole

A star that has the right amount of material left after its active life to form a white dwarf or neutron star will not later evolve into a black hole,[1] and, in terms of the evolution of stars, white dwarf and neutron stars do not really come before the black hole. Strictly speaking, the three types form three separate end-points of stellar evolution, although the first two forms, degenerate stars, so named because their highly compressed material has such high density, are before black holes in the sense that they represent less extreme states. Historically speaking, astronomy places the degenerate stars in conceptual terms as an end-point of stellar evolution (quite a different thing from Laplace's speculations.) White dwarf stars have been confirmed for decades and can be observed with ordinary telescopes; neutron stars were predicted in the thirties but were only discovered—quite unexpectedly—in 1967 when radio astronomers at the University of Cambridge detected pulsars.[2] Black-hole theory in its modern form, building from the idea of the collapse of dead stars, was developed almost in tandem with theories about neutron stars, but there is still lingering uncertainty as to whether a black hole actually has been found in space. Quite probably, future historians will accept one of the current crop of X-ray stars as a true black hole and set the date of the first identification of such an object as early as the seventies.

The difference between white dwarf stars, neutron stars, and stellar mass black holes (as viewed from outside the Schwarzschild radius) is only a difference of degree. It is not the existence of black holes as such that has caused a wave of excitement and speculation among mathematical astronomers during this decade, but the implication that within the black holes there might reside singularities, with the further implication that if black-hole singularities exist, then other kinds of singularities must also exist and play a powerful role in shaping the Universe as we know it and, perhaps, as we do not know it. Degenerate stars have provided a great deal of excitement for astronomers over the past ten or fifteen years and their story is worth telling.

The Binary Embrace

Almost without exception, the new astronomy, through which our understanding of the Universe has progressed since the early sixties, is high-energy astronomy. Explosive events within and outside our Galaxy, including exploding galaxies and debris from exploded white dwarf and neutron stars, provide information about the physical behavior of material under conditions quite different from those on Earth and quite impossible to reproduce in any laboratory. The only energy source that can power the violent events now known to be

NGC 5128. Peculiar galaxy. In Centaurus. Source of radio noise.
200-in. Hale.
Photograph from the Hale Observatories

common in the Universe is gravity—either involving very large masses, very dense objects, or both. In the case of the X-ray stars, there must also be a nearby companion star from which material can fall into the gravity well of the compact star where it heats up through the release of gravitational potential energy. How does a pair of stars get into such a state?

The discovery of X-ray stars had to await the development of sounding rockets and satellites that could carry X-ray detectors above the Earth's atmosphere, which screens out radiation of such high energies, but the theory of how such stars form is basic to the theory of stellar evolution developed decades ago. Although the first known X-ray star, Sco X-1, was discovered only in 1962, astrophysicists, using hindsight, now realize that a system in which one of two stars is a degenerate object at the end of its evolutionary life is the natural product of stellar evolution in close binary systems where two stars whirl about each other locked in a permanent gravitational embrace.

Very many ordinary stars exist in multiple systems—either binary or with two or more companions. It may even be that most stars occur in such systems and that the pattern of our Solar System—one sun and a scattering of planets—is not the norm. If two stars do form close together out of the same cloud of collapsing gas, it is unlikely that both will have even roughly the same

mass. The range between the masses of two stars in a binary system can be exampled in our own Solar System where the giant planet Jupiter has more than 300 times the mass of the Earth and is very nearly a star. With only slightly more mass, the core of Jupiter could be squeezed enough for nuclear fusion reactions to take place, and our Sun would have a small stellar companion. Jupiter is but one-thousandth the mass of the Sun. That is an extreme difference and Jupiter is not quite a star, but binary systems in which the ratio of the masses of the two stars is between 10 and 100 do occur, and, while the masses themselves cannot be measured directly from Earth, astronomers can accurately determine this mass ratio by measuring the changes in the optical appearance of the binary system caused by the orbital motion of the two stars. This method is governed by the same laws that Kepler found to apply to planets orbiting the Sun, which also provided Newton with the inspiration for much of his work on gravity.

A close pair of stars can exist quite happily for a long time without mutual interference, each evolving through its stellar life as nuclear fuel is burnt in the interior. It is known from studies of the many different kinds of stars in the Milky Way, in their many different stages of evolution, that after the first stage of evolution, when most of the original hydrogen has been fused into helium, the center contracts slightly and becomes hotter as new fusion reactions begin to convert helium into more complex elements. With the increase of heat inside, the outer parts of the star expand enormously; when the Sun reaches this stage (which won't be for a few million years yet), it will expand to engulf the Earth. Any close binary companion to a star entering this phase obviously is going to be affected.[3]

The bigger a star, the more quickly it will burn its nuclear fuel because it needs more energy to hold itself up against the insistent pull of its own gravity. So, in any binary pair, it is the star that was originally more massive that first expands and stretches out toward its partner. If the stars orbit each other closely enough, the smaller companion may then be able to acquire material by skimming off gas from its giant companion and, when this happens, the smaller star increases in mass, which increases its gravitational pull and enables it to skim off still more material from the larger star. In addition, the red giant will lose mass altogether, blowing gas outward into space in a stellar wind of particles. All stars, including our Sun, lose material in this way, but the loss is much greater for giant stars because the material at the surface of the star is already so far away from its center that gravity has only a weak grip on it and the escape velocity is low.

This brings about a curious situation. The larger star loses so much mass—both to interstellar space and to its companion—that it becomes smaller than the originally smaller companion. Now, the roles are reversed, with the previously secondary star going more rapidly through its evolutionary cycle, becoming a giant star and losing mass which can be captured by the original primary star, now small and compact. Detailed calculations of this kind of binary evolution have been made many times with the aid of high-speed electronic computers and, in a typical example, a pair of stars that start out as 22.6 and 2 solar masses respectively will evolve into a pair of 2 and 6.3 solar masses respectively by this second stage of evolution. As well as the roles being reversed, two thirds of the binary's original matter has been lost altogether. Just how small the compact star (the original primary) is by this stage depends very much on the details of the binary system. A white dwarf is easy to form from any star with the right amount of mass left once its nuclear fuel is spent; a neutron star is more likely to be formed when the central core of a giant star is compressed in a vast explosion—a supernova—which blasts away the remaining outer layers. And there is good evidence that all supernova explosions occur in binary systems, although no one really knows just what triggers off such an explosion.

Either way, the binary will exist for about a million years in the configuration where the former secondary, now a giant, dumps material onto its compact companion, whether it is a white dwarf or a neutron star. The transferred material does not fall directly onto the small companion but spirals inward and around it, creating a cloud of material about the compact star, which explains the erratic variability of such sources, as the cloud at times obscures the underlying X-ray source more than it does at other times. As we have seen, the compact object inside the cloud could be a black hole if the star leftover after all this swapping of matter has more than about three solar masses. The cloud of material would then funnel through a Schwarzschild throat; to an outside observer the difference would be one only of degree.

What happens after millions of years when the other star in the system reaches the end of its evolutionary trail? Perhaps the two compact objects would settle down into a quiet and neighborly old age, but, according to some calculations, the second star may explode with such violence that the entire system is disrupted and two neutron stars go hurtling away into space in different directions. This idea delights some astronomers since there are many high-velocity neutron stars in our Galaxy, which we detect as pulsars. It seems quite likely, on the other hand, that many, and probably most, pulsars have been singly produced, although it still requires a dramatic supernova explosion to compress a stellar remnant into the neutron star state. It is possible that the *initial* explosion is sometimes sufficient to disrupt the pair. Either way, pulsars do exist, and if they really are neutron stars, then they provide us with a view of matter at the greatest extreme of density in which it can exist without becoming a black hole.

Pulsars

The 1967 discovery of pulsars took the theorists by surprise. It had been known for thirty years that neutron stars theoretically should exist. It was known also that stars generally have magnetic fields, and it would have been but the work of a moment to estimate how fast a neutron star would spin after being formed, because the spin rate of a star increases as it contracts so as to conserve angular momentum in just the same way and following the same physical law that the spin of an ice skater increases as arm movement goes inward. But no one had had the imagination to envisage neutron stars as anything but cold, dead, degenerate stars sitting quietly in space and not interacting much with anything.[4]

There was high excitement in 1967 and 1968 over the discovery and interpretation of the signals from pulsars. The very rapid, precisely timed pulses of radiation were first identified as unusual by a graduate student, Jocelyn Bell (now Dr. Jocelyn Burnell) working with Professor Anthony Hewish's group at Cambridge; a story that the discovery was kept quiet for weeks because the scientists believed the signals might be coming from another intelligent civilization is not entirely true, since the prime objective in those weeks was to rule out the chance that the Cambridge radio telescope might be picking up interference from our own civilization. Still, the story contains some truth. It was certainly galling to theorists such as myself in those weeks late in 1967 and early in 1968 to know that my colleagues in radio astronomy had found something remarkable but were not telling just what it was.

The first few identified pulsars produced their pulses of radiation with periods close to a second; each pulsar has its own very precise period. Because of the precision and short duration of the pulses, it was clear that they must be coming from a source much smaller than a normal bright star. If the source were bigger than a small planet, the signal would be blurred out by an amount depending on the size of the source, just as the roar of a football crowd is blurred compared with the fainter but sharper sound of an individual voice. This limit on the size of the source was the origin of stories about signals from another civilization, but to astronomers it immediately implied that the pulsars must be white dwarf or neutron stars. As a young theorist faced with two possible explanations for the phenomenon and aware of the prospect of a niche in astronomical history for the person who first produced the "right" explanation, I plumped unhesitatingly for the white dwarf model—the "wrong" explanation! Professor Tommy Gold, already famous in 1968 as one of the originators of the Steady State Theory of the Universe and for other work, is now credited in the textbooks as having first suggested in a published paper that the rotation of neutron stars provided the most likely "clock mechanism" for the timing of pulsar pulses. Though apparently at a dead end, I was at least able to prove conclusively that no white dwarf model could possibly explain the variety of pulsars that had been found.

Optical and X-ray pulses have now been discovered for the most extreme source, in the Crab nebula, a neutron star spinning so quickly that its lighthouse beam flashes thirty times every second. The revival of interest in degenerate stars, which the discovery of pulsars triggered off, also had direct relevance to the development of theories about X-ray stars.

At the Heart of Matter

The discovery of matter in its degenerate state before the black hole has alone provided a major contribution to the new astronomy of high energies. Although the neutron star is still accepted as the ultimate state of dense matter, there has been one development in the mid-seventies which suggests that, by pushing the definition of neutron star a bit, astrophysics can provide a new insight into the nature of matter itself and reveal something more than before about the very origin of all the matter we know—the origin of the Universe.

The idea of the atom as the indivisible, fundamental building block of matter appeared in ancient Greece, only to be lost and reintroduced more than two thousand years later. As the feasibility of small-scale scientific experiments increased, it became clear that atoms could be divided into negatively charged electrons and positively charged nuclei. Theorists then developed a model of the structure of atoms which suggested that the heretofore supposed indivisible nuclei were made up of two further kinds of elementary particles, positively charged protons and electrically neutral neutrons. In reality, splitting the atom means splitting the nucleus. Experimenters confirmed this new model as being a good approximation to reality and opened the way for the practical development of nuclear energy from fission. Throughout the late fifties and sixties, experimenters produced a shoal of further fundamental particles by smashing these basic particles of the atom together in giant accelerators. The question raised by all this smashing of not just atoms but even of so-called fundamental particles is whether *any* particles can really be regarded as fundamental and indivisible. Current thinking postulates that such genuinely indivisible particles do exist, named quarks, and that the myriad of fundamental particles found so far are all made up of quarks in the same way that atoms are made of particles more fundamental than atoms. The concept is reminiscent of the old rhyme,

> Big fleas have little fleas
> upon their backs to bite 'em;
> and little fleas have smaller fleas,
> and so ad infinitum.

Prologue 2: Before the Black Hole

So far no one has produced unequivocal experimental proof that quarks do exist. Still, if they do, imagine what would happen to a neutron star so massive that at the center neutrons are not just pressed tight alongside each other but begin to be squeezed into one another in some way. The density needed for such a process would be more than 1,000-million million grams per cubic centimeter, equivalent to what someone once described as ten large ocean liners squeezed to the size of a pin head. If neutrons and all other fundamental particles actually are made up of quarks, then, at such a level of compression the neutrons would have to lose their individual identity and be replaced by a soup of quarks, in just the same way that in transition from white dwarf to neutron star densities individual atomic nuclei lose their identities and become replaced by a soup of neutrons. Though this may prove to be the ultimate state of density, there may—if past experience is anything to go by—be still littler "fleas" to be identified. However, even the quark soup cannot stop the collapse of a sufficiently massive star into a black hole; the new theory tells us more about the intermediate conditions between ordinary matter and the singularity—if, that is, the black hole singularity actually occurs. At the other end of the space-time spectrum, the quark soup theory tells us more about conditions close to another singularity, one we know existed, the birth of the Universe.

According to conventional ideas, the Universe began in a Big Bang, an outburst of material from a singularity. By winding the clock back, physical theories can be made to tell us a lot about the early state of the Universe when all the material in space was much closer together. Indeed—if you are prepared to accept a few assumptions—the theorists can offer quite a good account of the history of the Universe since the time that it had the density of a neutron star. This description can now be extended back to the time when everything was compressed into one lump at the density of quark soup—a lump just thirty kilometers across and containing everything in the Universe as we know it. This would be a time just one ten-thousandth of a second after the Universe began its expansion from a literally infinite density in a point singularity. What all cosmologists would like to know, of course, is just what happened during the first ten-thousandth of a second, even before the quark soup was formed, and that is far from being the least important reason for the study of singularities.

Although the circumstantial evidence is strong, the black-hole singularity remains not quite proven. However, the Universe does exist; it has expanded and blasted out and away from the original creation event. We also see outward explosions in many smaller scale events scattered across the present-day Universe. Under such conditions, it is surely sensible to consider the study of singularities in the context of outward explosions, cosmic gushers, the white holes of creation. And where better to begin than with the study of the origin of the expanding Universe in the greatest conceivable cosmic gusher?

Part I
Where Do We Come From?

1

THE BIG BANG AND THE EXPANDING UNIVERSE

The most fundamental astronomical observation is that night follows day. Although it was not realized until the eighteenth century and not widely publicized until the nineteenth, that single observation is enough to tell us that the Universe expands. It hints strongly that creation occurred at a definite time in the past, in the cosmic gusher of the Big Bang. How can a dark Universe be full of bright stars? This question is the essence of Olbers' paradox, named after the German astronomer Heinrich Wilhelm Olbers (1758–1840) who published a discussion of it in 1826. (Unknown to Olbers it had previously been dealt with by de Cheseaux in 1744.) Put at its simplest, Olbers' paradox states that, if the Universe is infinite in extent and goes on forever in all directions, and if there are stars throughout that infinite Universe, then in every direction we look, our line of sight must intersect with a star. Therefore, every point of the night sky should be bright.

What the Dark Sky Means

If we imagine a thin spherical shell of a given radius surrounding a point in a uniform universe of stars, we can work out the average brightness of starlight in the thin shell that would be seen by an observer at the center of the sphere. On a smaller scale, to an observer at the Earth's center the thin layer of atmosphere on the Earth's surface would appear as such a spherical shell. Because we are positing a situation in which the density of stars is uniform, the number of stars within the shell would depend only on the volume of the shell which would be directly proportional to the square of the radius of the sphere, that is, to the square of the distance to the central observer. But the apparent intensity of a light source decreases with distance in exactly the same way as the square of the distance, with the curious result that shells of the same thickness would look equally bright to the central observer—they would contribute equally to the brightness of the night sky—regardless of their radii. It seems that the effect of this would be an infinitely bright night sky, since for an infinite Universe there would be an infinite number of shells, each contributing the same finite amount of light, but there is another factor to take into account: the nearer stars block out some of the light from the distant stars be-

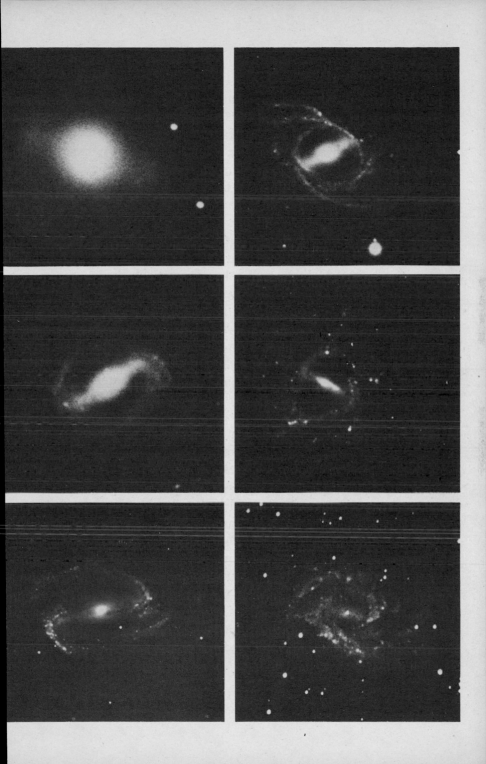

hind them. When this is allowed for, the resultant brightness of the night sky ought to be "merely" the brightness at the surface of an average star—about 40,000 times the brightness of the Sun at noon. So Olbers' paradox presents not just the phenomenon of a dark night sky—it is as much of a puzzle that the sky should be relatively so dark in the day as well.

Obviously, there is something wrong with the cosmological theory on which these estimates are based. At the time of de Cheseaux and Olbers, it was accepted that the Universe must be uniform, unchanging, and static and that stars had always existed in an infinite Universe, looking much the same at all times, with no universal motion. By providing this simple observational test, Olbers' paradox proved unequivocally that this picture of the Universe was wrong and provided the beginning of an observational cosmology that led to the development of a new world picture.

There is much evidence that the Universe is, on the grand scale, uniform in terms of distribution of the galaxies of stars, and there is some evidence, as we shall see later, that the Universe is changing and evolving, but the kind of change we are able to see does not remove the problem of Olbers' paradox. Thus the third assumption of Olbers' time, that the Universe is static, must be rejected in the light—that is, the dark—of the paradox. Following this acceptance, the Doppler effect can be used to show why the sky is dark at night.

As distance between the source of sound or light and observer becomes less or greater, frequency of waves received increases or decreases respectively, giving rise to the effect known as the Doppler effect. For example, in sound, the pitch of a siren on a fast-moving vehicle moving away from the listener will deepen. A light source moving away from the viewer will weaken because its wave length is stretched causing a shift of color toward the red end of the spectrum. Thus, the faster the light source (of star or galaxy) recedes, the weaker its light will become. With the further shells of stars moving away from the observer faster than the nearer ones, only nearby shells contribute much light to the sky and the influence of more distant shells weakens in proportion to their distance from us.

This is a very powerful, basic conclusion to emerge from a simple observation, as Herman Bondi has stressed, "It is a peculiarity of our universe that it is dark and cold but contains very hot bright bodies, the stars."[1] In thermodynamics, we know that such differences tend to average out; ice cubes dropped in hot water will, for example, melt while the water will be cooled. In thermodynamic terms, if the Universe has been around for a long time, then there should have been a strong tendency for the hot brightness of the stars to become dissipated in the cold darkness of space, to a point approaching thermodynamic equilibrium. Perhaps the Universe is relatively young, but certainly any good theory of it must explain that it is not today in thermodynamic equilibrium. To quote Bondi again, "Thermodynamic properties tend to be very deep and significant: the fact that our night sky is very black, with very bright points, the stars, in it, may be the profoundest piece of knowledge of the universe that we have."[2]

If the density of the Universe, in terms of the number of galaxies occupying a given volume of space, is decreasing today, then to run the film backward, as it were, would be to look farther and farther into the past to a Universe of increasing density. Ultimately, watching the Universe unfolding backward we would see matter squeezed together at very high densities, with galaxies, stars, atomic nuclei, and even quarks, crushed out of existence and disappearing into a singularity. This is, of course, the familiar story of a high-density black hole, expanded to encompass the entire Universe, but it is also the story of our Universe told *in reverse*. If the Universe has been expanding since the moment of creation, in order to reach its present state it would have been created as a massive singularity—a white hole— bursting outward with quarks, neutron stars, and galaxies being born. This is a profound piece of knowledge indeed; anyone who doubts the reality of white holes also is doubting the origin and existence of the Universe.

Mathematician Roger Penrose, discussing the possibility that there might be naked singularities, that is, those not hidden behind an event horizon and with which we can interact, points out that the Big Bang was itself naked. If other singularities can be investigated, they may tell us more about conditions near the origin of the Universe. Equally, an understanding of the Big Bang tells us what to expect from smaller scale singularities.

"The initial mystery of creation," says Penrose, "would no longer be able to hide in the obscurity afforded by its supposed uniqueness. . . ,"[3] if other naked singularities could be found. Since one of the least satisfactory features of the Big Bang theory is that it cannot explain the origin of the Universe, this is of the greatest importance. Also, philosophically it is no more satisfying to say that the Universe appeared in a Big Bang than to say that the Universe was created in the form we now see it. The fact that we can explain—or think we can explain—how the Universe changed from a quark soup thirty kilometers in diameter to its present state does not solve the fundamental mystery of creation either, but it changes the question to, where did the quark soup come from?

Posing such questions brings the cosmologist close to areas of thought more commonly associated with philosophy and religion—small wonder that there is a Chair at the University of Cambridge, "Plumian Professor of Astronomy and Experimental Philosophy."

Curiously, some of the theories of the origin of the Universe reported in Genesis coincide with modern scientific thought. Science-fiction readers sometimes debate which is the oldest science-fiction story. There are many candidates, and the debate will probably never be resolved, but, given the cosmology and astronomy of the time, the authors of Genesis surely qualify as among the earliest science-fiction speculators. From a judicious selection of apposite verses, a case could be made for the ancients' superior knowledge, now lost. Genesis offers evidence as good as any yet published that the Earth was visited by space travelers thousands of years ago. The account of the creation in Genesis could be a garbled version of the cosmology taught by these outerspace visitors.

And God said, Let there be light: and there was light.

Clearly this refers to the beginning of the Universe in a white hole.

And God saw the light, that it was good: and God divided the light from the darkness.

This is a remarkable reference to the expansion of the Universe, which, as we know, is the reason for the dark night sky.

Other references indicate the order of evolution both of and on the Earth—first the seas formed, then dry land; life evolved in the oceans and moved onto the land; plants appeared before animal life; Man came last.

Hindsight is a marvelous aid in putting thoughts into the minds of others and to profound interpretations of simple sentences. As with other interpretations of the visits from outer space, the first question is, what is the content of the material which is not quoted? Unfortunately, but hardly surprisingly, the rest of Genesis does not provide remarkable insights into cosmic gushers, and I do not seriously offer the suggestion that it was written by students of space visitors. Nonetheless, this early and perceptive attempt to offer a theory of the origin of the Universe beyond "God created everything," by spelling out the order and relative time-scale of the process, indicates how deeply rooted is human curiosity about the creation. As cosmology covers much of what was once a matter of faith, until the development of new observational facilities in this century, it is not surprising that some of its controversies have taken on the aspects of a religious war.

The Steady State Alternatives

In the fifties, an alternative to the Big Bang theory became popular. This is the Steady State theory and its origin was initially more philosophical than astronomical. The idea of the Big Bang is disturbing to those who ask, what came before the Big Bang and why did it explode? The answer to both questions is that we don't know. One way around this is to suggest that there never was a Big Bang, and it is possible to do this while avoiding Olbers' paradox, provided one is prepared to accept the idea of a continual creation of matter. However, to accept that is difficult for one indoctrinated by the teachings and experiences of physics on Earth where matter is conserved. In more sophisticated terms, matter means mass/energy. The Steady State theory requires the *creation* of mass/energy. Philosophically, is it more difficult to believe that matter is created continually in small dribbles throughout the Universe than it is to believe that all the matter in the Universe was created at a singular fixed moment in time?

The Steady State theory originated in the forties from the independent approach of Bondi and Gold, working together, and of Fred Hoyle. Hoyle and his later colleagues, including especially J. V. Narlikar, based the theory on a modification of the equations of the general theory of relativity. The Bondi-Gold approach, however, was almost entirely deductive and was based on a central principle, the so-called Perfect Cosmological Principle. Here is where the philosophy comes in. Before Bondi and Gold, cosmologists had already used a cosmological principle in the form of a statement that the Universe is essentially isotropic, that is, the same in all directions, and homogeneous, that is, having the same view from all points within it. This may be a hangover from the earlier idea of a uniform Universe, but this cosmological principle describes uniformity only in space. With Big Bang cosmology, the Universe clearly looks different at different epochs. The Perfect Cosmological Principle, on the other hand, goes further and states that the Universe is essentially unchanging in time as well as in space.

The philosophical basis for this is plausible and, intuitively at least, very attractive. All our study of the Universe depends on the interpretation of observations of such phenomena as radio, light, and other electromagnetic waves and of cosmic rays, all of which come from distant parts of the Universe. Such interpretations are made on the assumption that the laws of physics applicable to galaxies and stars which emit radiation are the same laws of physics governing the Earth and its Solar System. If such is not the case, astronomy and cosmology are futile pursuits, but what kind of a law of physics requires the laws of physics themselves to be absolutely universal? The best guess is that in some way the overall structure of the Universe itself determines the laws of physics, which then have universal application. In that case, the only way to ensure that those laws have always applied is to assume that the Universe, if viewed on a large enough scale, has always been the same as it is today.

Taken together with Olbers' paradox, the Perfect Cosmological Principle tells us that the Universe must always expand yet always show the same overall appearance. If the expansion is not to produce a decrease in the universal density of galaxies, then this, in turn, implies that new matter must be created to fill the gaps left by expansion. In other words, although given enough time the distance between the local group of galaxies to which the Milky Way belongs and the nearest separate group will double, over the same time-scale a complete new group of galaxies must be created in the gap to preserve the same overall view from the Milky Way. As we know from the measured expansion rate of the Universe, the rate of creation needed is very small—one hydrogen atom appearing in a volume of one liter each 1,000,000 million years, which is about 100 times longer than the age of the entire Universe on the Big Bang theory! The Steady State theory has always been aesthetically pleasing, for it removes the problem of creation by holding that the Universe always was and always will be. It requires that the laws of physics be identical everywhere in the Universe at all times. If it also requires that tiny amounts of matter be created, by regarding the Universe as an entity it offers an explanation of how a hydrogen atom "knows" when and where to be created. There is the problem of arranging the new hydrogen atoms into stars and galaxies, but there are also real problems with theories of galaxy formation in the Big Bang universe.

One idea that the proponents of the Steady State theory offered was that new material might be created in regions of high density, at the centers of already existing galaxies, and explode outward into the universe to condense later into new stars and galaxies. This picture of galactic gushers is not unlike the best theories of how galaxies formed after the Big Bang, and we shall return to the theme shortly. The greatest strength of the Steady State theory, however, was always its simplicity, which encouraged observations aimed at testing it; and by the mid-sixties hope of retaining the theory in its basic, aesthetically uncomplicated form seemed to have been ruled out.

From Our Point in Time

The tests depended on pushing our observations of the Universe to greater and greater distances by using radio astronomy techniques and counts of the numbers of galaxies and radio sources at various distances from us. From this evidence it appears that the Universe is not unchanging in time. When we look at the electromagnetic radiation from distant sources, we are, in effect, looking backward in time, since even at a speed of 30,000 million centimeters a second, light and radio waves take millions of years to reach us from distant galaxies.[4] Thus, the counts of sources at different distances, based on samples of old light, are really snapshots indicating the density of the galaxies in the Universe at different times in its history, and they show, not absolutely but very suggestively, that as it expands, the Universe is evolving from a denser to a less dense state, rendering the Perfect Cosmological Principle invalid.

For an ardent Steady Stater, there are ways round this. Hoyle and Narlikar, for example, argued in the mid-sixties that our Universe might be uniform in time and space and that our expanding, thinning region of space might be simply a local, temporary, insignificant universal fluctuation—a bubble thousands of millions of light-years across in a still greater sea.

However, any tinkering with the basic simplicity of the Steady State theory is self-defeating; by tacking odd bits onto the theory we make it less attractive than the simpler Big Bang explanation. When the argument is boiled down to the suggestion that the Universe as we see it seems like it started in a Big Bang, because we are living in a part of a Steady State universe which just happens to be indistinguishable from a Big Bang universe, it is as if we were not considering whether Shakespeare's plays might have been written by Francis Bacon, but whether they were in fact written by another man called William Shakespeare who just happens to be indistinguishable from the accredited author. The Big Bang–Steady State controversy continues in a modified form, with the important difference that the Steady Staters remaining have become supporters of the idea that the Universe is a complicated place. Narlikar has said, "My own belief is that the structure of the universe is much more interesting and sophisticated than that suggested by either the Big Bang model or the Steady State model."[5] By definition, however, the Big Bang model encompasses and allows for a certain degree of complication which the Steady State theory of the Perfect Cosmological Principle does not.

The Echo of Creation

The crucial evidence in favor of the Big Bang model does not come from complicating factors but from the simplest and most obvious test of all: radio astronomers can observe the Big Bang. The dying echo of the greatest cosmic gusher can be detected as a faint hiss of radio noise coming from all directions in space—the blackbody background radiation at a temperature of 2.7 degrees absolute (−270°C.). It is even more remarkable that the discovery itself was made by accident in 1965 and was interpreted by a new generation of astronomers, although this background noise was a direct prediction of the idea of a hot Big Bang origin of the Universe discussed by theorists thirty years ago.

The first observations of the cosmic background noise were made in 1965 by two radio astronomers, Arno Penzias and Robert Wilson, working for Bell Laboratories. The sound coming from all directions in space was about 100 times louder than that which should result from the smoothed-out effect of all the distant sources of radio noise in radio galaxies and similar objects. Although the discovery came as a surprise to Penzias and Wilson, it was immediately understood by their neighbor at Princeton University, Robert Dicke. Having independently developed the idea of a hot Big Bang first proposed by George Gamow in the forties, Dicke was building a receiver to search for just that kind of background sound. The theory of a hot Big Bang origin of the Universe predicts the background radio noise, since, like any other hot body, the primordial Universe would radiate electromagnetic energy according to Planck's "black-body" law. Very early in the history of the Universe there would have been a strong interaction between matter and radiation but, by about 100 seconds after the outburst from the singularity, matter and radiation should have decoupled to lead independent lives thereafter. The expanding Universe would dilute the residual radiation with the radiation losing energy and effectively cooling so that now, 10,000 million years later, it would correspond to a black-body spectrum at a mere three degrees absolute, far faded from its initial glory of 1,000 million degrees. Another way to look at it is that the radiation has red shifted by an enormous factor. Either view points to the same conclusion: the Universe did originate in a Big Bang and is not in a steady state.

Other Universal Perspectives

If, therefore, the Perfect Cosmological Principle is not relevant to the real Universe, the way opens to speculate that the laws of physics have not been the same throughout history. Ironically, Fred Hoyle, the most die-hard proponent of the Steady State theory, has taken advantage of this to propose new theories involving physical constants which change with time. Though this smacks of hedging, there is no denying that Hoyle has some novel ideas. One suggests that, instead of a universal expansion, there may be a situation in which the mass of everything in the Universe has increased from zero since a time approximately 15,000 million years ago, usually regarded as the moment of the Big Bang. The effect of this changing mass on the light from distant objects (which, remember, we see as if they were in the distant past) is to produce a red shift and remove Olbers' paradox; the light from a hydrogen atom with less mass than the hydrogen atoms in our laboratories on Earth will be shifted in accordance with the Doppler effect. With this new model, we can extend back beyond the time ordinarily considered the beginning of the Universe to a time in which the masses of atoms and everything else are negative. If, further back still, further away in space, there are regions of positive mass, we are back to a kind of Steady State universe in which our local region just happens to look as if it were created in a

Big Bang. It's a stimulating intellectual exercise, but I prefer the standard Big Bang cosmology which, in spite of opposition from a variety of exotic cosmologies, has persisted as a viable explanation of the real Universe for more than fifty years.

There have been ironies and peculiarities associated with the development of the Big Bang cosmology, not least because of a blunder by Einstein which unnecessarily complicated his presentation of the equations describing the Universe and which, incidentally, seems not to have taken Olbers' paradox into account. The equations of the general theory of relativity can be applied to describe the behavior of large aggregations of matter, including the whole Universe, but the simplest application of these equations gives a solution allowing for either universal expansion or universal contraction but unable to accommodate a static Universe. Sixty years ago this looked embarrassing since it was generally accepted (in spite of Olbers' paradox) that the Universe was static. In order to allow for static solutions of the equations, Einstein introduced an extra fiddle-factor, the so-called cosmological constant, so that he could predict the existence of a static universe to satisfy the equations and also introduce effects corresponding to the presence of matter. Hoyle and Narlikar, in particular, were to make great use of the opportunities provided by the cosmological constant in their construction of exotic Steady State cosmologies within (more or less) the overall framework of the general theory of relativity. But, in 1917, de Sitter showed that Einstein's field equations could be solved without an extra factor to describe the presence of mass (zero cosmological constant), and he showed that the solution gave an empty, expanding universe.

That is not quite as baffling as it sounds. There is much more empty space than there is matter in our Universe. A few negligibly small particles (the galaxies) participate in the universal expansion. The snag was that, in 1917, apart from Olbers' paradox, there was no direct evidence that the Universe did expand. So the Einstein–de Sitter model, as it is known, languished for some time as one of many solutions to the field equations. Being, however, the simplest solution, it should have been taken more seriously than most; one of the gratifying features of cosmology is that, for once, it seems that the simplest interpretation of the equations explains the behavior of the real Universe.

Still, it is hardly surprising that imaginative cosmologists of fifty years ago balked at a set of equations purporting to describe the behavior of a universe consisting only of empty space. This is so far from being common sense that even science-fiction imagination cannot encompass the concept.

As theorists have developed cosmology and mathematicians have developed equations describing space-time, it has ironically become more and more questionable as to just how real solid matter is. As we shall see later, the currently favored imaginative view is that everything can be explained in terms of curved space and, while most people are still struggling to overcome their prejudices, the most imaginative members of the scientific community are today quite happy with the concept of a universe containing only curved and empty (but expanding) space. What the present-day commonsense view still tells us is that empty space may in fact be the basic, textured fabric of the Universe on which matter is carried along and through which black and white holes make tunnels.

In view of Einstein's misguided introduction of the cosmological constant, there is greater irony in the cosmology story—we don't even need relativity theory to produce a set of equations describing the behavior of the whole Universe, including its expansion. Using Newtonian physics alone it is quite possible to produce a cosmology with all the subtlety of the relativistic version (including a Newtonian version of the cosmological constant and a Newtonian Steady State model). Although Newtonian cosmology was developed not by Newton but only after relativistic cosmology was developed in the early part of this century, it is largely equivalent to the relativistic cosmology as a tool for describing the Universe. The laws of motion governing a universal fluid in which pressure and density vary only with time are the same for both Newtonian and Einsteinian mechanics, and this again is very persuasive evidence that these laws of motion provide a fundamental insight into what is happening in the Universe. Since the solution of the equations involves integration, which introduces another unknown constant, this insight is not unique, even without the cosmological constant. Setting Einstein's cosmological constant at zero (which is overwhelmingly the sensible thing to do with an unnecessary constant), the behavior of the model cosmological universe will be different depending on whether the genuine constant of integration is zero, positive, or negative. Both the first and last possibilities, however, provide models which expand away from a point of singularity at some definite time in the past and continue expanding forever; the odd-man-out is the model with a positive constant of integration which expands away from a point but then, after some finite time, slows down, stops, and collapses back into a singularity. This bouncing model has some interesting implications, which we shall dwell on at length later, arising principally from the fact that after the collapse there is nothing to exclude another phase of expansion and collapse, with infinitely repeated bounces.

The Range of Models

Though the cosmological constant has been discredited, it is entertaining to review the great diversity of universes that could exist through the equations of both Newtonian and Einsteinian mechanics. By introducing another constant, each of the three basic models becomes split into three further alternatives depending on whether the new constant is zero, positive, or negative. Though there are further subgroups possible, because some of the classes are quite similar to one another, six basic families are left. There are no fewer than five different versions of the monotonically expanding models, those starting from a singularity and expanding away forever, and four versions of the model which oscillates between a singularity and some finite size. One curious model starts out from a finite size and begins expanding indefinitely, while a counterpart starts out from a singularity but tends ever closer toward a definite size without ever quite reaching it, the expansion becoming slower and slower as the limiting size is approached ever more closely. The most curious model is the completely static one that caused the introduction of the cosmological constant in the first place. One of the most entertaining possibilities is a model in which the universe contracts from infinity to a finite size and then expands away again to infinity. All the models, except the static one, include an expanding phase, so on that evidence alone any one could be the correct analogy of the real Universe. But these are unnecessary complications. Better to wait until someone proves that the simplest model of universal expansion from a singularity is not correct. That will be time enough to ponder on more complicated possibilities.

Although the bouncing models are of particular importance and will come into their own in Part III of this book, they are so commonly referred to, even in science fiction, and so often incorrectly described, that one ought to look at them in a little more detail. The expansion-followed-by-collapse models are, of course, almost as simple as the straightforward, continuously expanding models; if complication is to be introduced, this is a likely direction for it to take. It is very important, however, to realize that the collapse back to a singularity is not something involving matter alone but is a collapse of the whole fabric of space-time, just as the expansion is an expansion of the fabric of space-time. There is no way in which an observer might stay outside the collapse in a space ship and watch all the material of the Universe gather together in a singularity and then explode outward again (as the crew of the space ship *Leonora Christine* do in Poul Anderson's novel, *Tau Zero*), because there is no outside from which to make the observations. Indeed, the equations which produce the descriptive model universes of both Newtonian and Einsteinian mechanics take very little account of matter at all. We are essentially talking about an empty universe in which it is the fabric of space-time that expands or contracts, with odd bits of matter being carried along like so much flotsam in a fast-flowing current. In a very simple analogy, we might consider galaxies represented by a row of evenly spaced dots on a strip of rubber; if the rubber is put under tension and stretched, the dots (galaxies) move farther apart, but they have not moved through the fabric of the rubber (space-time). If we squeeze the rubber, screw it up, burn it, or whatever, the dots inevitably are subjected to the same process. The destruction of space-time in a singularity carries the matter to the same fate; the dots do not flow through the fabric of the rubber to congregate at one end leaving the unaltered fabric behind.

Was there really a Big Bang? As recently as 1971, Geoffrey Burbidge was pondering this question in an article in *Nature*:[6]

> I believe that the answer clearly must be that we do not know, and that if we are ever to find an answer much more effort must be devoted to cosmological tests, with a much more open-minded approach, and that much more original thinking must be done to attempt to explain the large amount of observational material, and not only material that can be used in a narrow sense to fit preconceived ideas.

Clearly, feelings still run high in the cosmological debate, and although I do not go along unreservedly with what

Burbidge says, it is important to realize that there is still a school of thought that does not accept the certainty of the Big Bang theory of the origin of the Universe. Still, suggestions like those of Hoyle and Narlikar that a new physics is needed to explain the observed phenomena of the Universe seem to me to go too far. We can indeed explain the overall features of the Universe by a Big Bang, as the greatest white hole of all, and we can further explain much of the "large amount of observational material" to which Burbidge refers, not by invoking the new physics of Hoyle and Narlikar, but by sticking with the same equations of energetic expansion —describing the white hole phenomenon—that we are used to in describing the whole Universe. This approach to the puzzles of the Universe produces some surprises and some laws of physics which seem quite new compared with those that govern everyday events here on Earth. But they are not new—simply the old physics applied to a new area. But before examining these new applications of the old physics a quick overview of some of that observational material is needed to give some idea of the state of the Universe today.

2
PERCEPTIONS FROM
INSIDE THE BALLOON

Seen with hindsight, the dark night sky shows that we live in an expanding Universe. Einstein himself did not find that evidence sufficient, but we now have additional evidence from diverse sources. Historically, the discovery of the red shifts and their interpretations in terms of the Doppler effect thought to be caused by an expanding Universe is the evidence which swung the weight of cosmological opinion away from the idea of a static universe for which Einstein fiddled his cosmological equations. As we have seen, the ultimate proof that the Universe is not only expanding but originated in a hot Big Bang came only a decade ago with the discovery of cosmic background radiation—the echo of the Big Bang itself. This convinced all but a handful of Steady State theorists that the picture of our Universe as the product of a cosmic white hole gushing outward is correct.

Background radiation (so named because it comes from all directions in space) permeates the entire Universe, but at any one place it is very slight. A weak hiss of radio noise, equivalent to the electromagnetic radiation from a black body at a temperature of only 2.7 K

$(-270.3\,^{\circ}\text{C})$, it may seem a feeble manifestation of the wonders of the Universe compared to the dramatic energy of quasars, pulsars, and X-ray stars. Yet this faint hiss provides direct evidence of the most dramatic, energetic event in the Universe. Detected best at frequencies between 1 megahertz and 500 megahertz, the radiation is that weak today only because the Universe has grown so large since it burst from the primordial singularity. One way of looking at it is as the result of an extreme red shifting of the original radiation. Another is that it has simply been diluted as the Universe has grown, since it must always have completely filled the total volume of the Universe, and that volume has increased from zero to its present vastness over the past 15,000 million years or so. Even for radiation with energy corresponding to a black-body temperature of 2.7 K (the temperature at which an ideal radiator would produce exactly the same kind of spectrum in the heat it radiated), the total radiation over the universal vastness gives an impressive amount of energy. Using the most widely known of all Einstein's equations, $E=mc^2$, but turned on its head to give $m=E/c^2$, we can relate that energy to an equivalent amount of matter. The surprising result of adding up all of the energy in the background radiation throughout the Universe and converting it into a mass equivalent is that as much energy resides in this feeble hiss of radio noise as the mass energy of all the

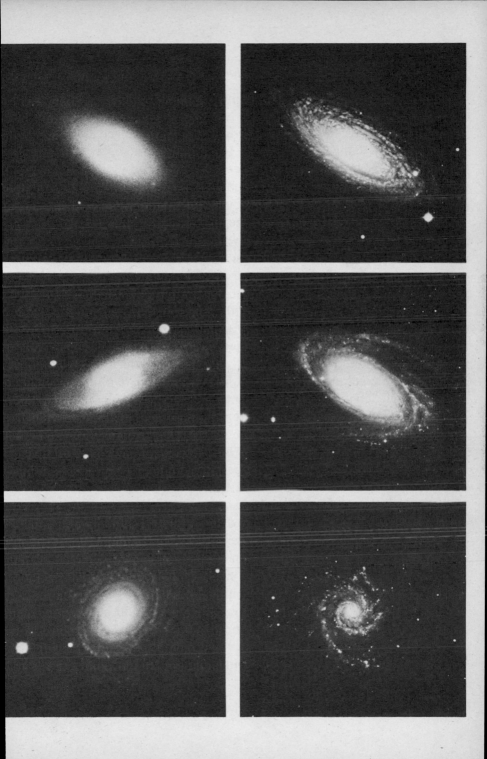

bright stars in all the bright galaxies put together. Therefore, in cosmic terms the background is quite significant.

In reconsidering the evolution of the Universe since it first burst into existence from a white hole, we should bear in mind the influence of this background radiation —so far the neglected part of the story. In looking at the expansion it is necessary to choose arbitrarily some starting point, not from zero volume and infinite density (which cannot be coped with by our present understanding of physics), but at some time shortly after the beginning of the expansion. Our best cosmological and physical theories are reliable guides to what the Universe must have been like at that time when it had cooled only to about a 1,000,000 million degrees absolute (K) and had expanded sufficiently for the so-called elementary particles to have appeared and to have begun to interact in accordance with the laws that we see at work in atom-smashing experiments in giant accelerators today. As we have seen, the very latest theories may tell us about times when the Universe was the hot, dense quark soup which had not evolved enough for the familiar elementary particles known to atomic physics as protons, neutrons, and electrons to have formed.

At 1,000,000 million degrees (10^{12} K), particles and radiation would be just about interchangeable; in the primordial fireball, particles and radiation would constantly be annihilated and created, although the total energy overall of the combined radiation-matter soup would be constant. At only one-tenth of that temperature (a mere 10^{11} K), however, things would begin to be more orderly, with the more bizarre forms of elementary particles no longer being produced because the density of the radiation at every point in the Universe would have become too small. At lower temperatures, only electrons and positrons could still be involved in annihilation and creation exchanges with their equivalent energies in the form of electromagnetic radiation. Protons and neutrons would have settled down in the numbers that exist today. According to the laws of physics, antiprotons and anti-neutrons had as much chance of being produced as their counterparts, and there is nothing in those laws to rule out the possibility that some of the galaxies we see in the sky are made up of antimatter, with positively charged electrons, negatively charged protons, and anti-neutrons combining to make up the antiatoms in their antistars, antiplanets, and even antipeople. If matter and antimatter should come into contact, both would be destroyed as their entire rest mass converted into energy as radiation; however, the spaces between the galaxies— or, at least, between clusters of galaxies—are so great that we cannot tell whether our neighbors are made of matter or antimatter, and the spaces are sufficient to keep opposite forms separate, preventing mutual annihilation. Since the laws of physics seem to be symmetrical, it may well be that just half of the material of the Universe is composed of matter and the other half of antimatter, and that both are rather lumpily distributed in the uneven patches we see as galaxies. Perhaps it was only the expansion of the Universe that stopped all of this material from coming into annihilating contact, which would have left a Universe composed of nothing except background radiation. Or perhaps, just by chance or through some unsuspected asymmetry in the physics of the fireball, the material of the present-day Universe is all matter of the kind we have in our Solar System, with no antimatter anywhere. In that picture, the deficiency of material in the Universe and the presence of so much empty space (empty except for background radiation) is no surprise; rather, the surprise is that there is any solid matter at all. Our planet, our stars, and ourselves may be garbage left over from the great cleanout by the fire of the Big Bang.

Nonetheless, there *is* matter in the Universe and the same matter must have been present as the expansion cooled things down from an overall 10^{11} K to a temperature only one-hundredth as great, 10^9 K (1,000 million degrees). This cooling was particularly significant, for below that temperature the radiation density became too small for even electron-positron pairs to be produced. All the pairs that could get together were annihilated once and for all; a relatively few electrons were left over, at least in our region of space. Perhaps a few positrons were left over in other regions of the Universe, but, at this point, the *major* links between material and radiation had been broken—the two great entities decoupled and continued to evolve along their almost independent paths within the expanding Universe. For matter, this is where the story really begins. While the temperature remained near 10^9 K, protons and neutrons could combine to form helium nuclei, although, with continued expansion, the temperature dropped and this fusion (the same nuclear fusion process that provides the energy of the Sun) ceased. At around 5,000 K, the protons and helium nuclei at last got together with the electrons to form atoms of hydrogen and helium. Since neutral atoms are scarcely affected by radiation, this stage of universal evolution signaled the end of the last remaining links between matter and radiation. From now on, the radiation could only cool down and spread out to keep the expanding Universe full. Five thousand degrees may seem weak compared with 1,000,000 million degrees, but the decline of the background radiation into decrepit old age continued to the 2.7 K we detect today and the cooling will continue as the Universe continues to expand, creeping ever closer to absolute zero, but never quite reaching it.[1]

The Problem of Measurement

The surface of our Sun, which is at a temperature of about 5,000 K, is in a state very similar to that of the whole Universe at the time when matter and radiation completely decoupled. The surface of the Sun is by everyday standards a fair example of a fiery furnace— but in cosmic terms those conditions represent the dying flicker of the original cosmic fireball. To study more recent events, we are stuck with the yardstick of cosmological red shifts, which is by no means a perfect tool and may be just as inappropriate as using a meter rule to measure temperatures.

It was only fifty or so years ago that astronomers first knew for sure that the spectacular Milky Way formed by our own Galaxy is but a minor part of the cosmological scene, and that beyond the Milky Way there are many other galaxies of multitudinous shapes and sizes, each, perhaps, as spectacular and important to its inhabitants (if they exist) as the Milky Way is to us. Before the twenties, it had been suspected that various forms of nebulae existed in the heavens, and there had been speculation that these objects—or at least some of them —might be whole galaxies lying beyond the Milky Way and, because of their great distances, appearing only as faint wisps in telescopic observations. The question was finally settled when observations with the great 100-inch telescope at Mount Wilson resolved some of these nebulae into component stars whose distances could be measured.

How can the distances to stars be measured, even within the Milky Way? The chain of innuendo that astronomers use to infer the distances of the most remote cosmological objects is far from being as strong as one would like. It depends on many linked assumptions about the properties of matter, and most of all it depends on the basic assumption that the laws of physics are as equally applicable to distant galaxies as they are to Earth and the stars of the Milky Way. As a result of the parallax effect produced by the movement of the Earth in its orbit around the Sun, stellar distances to our nearest neighbors—on the cosmic scale of things—can be measured directly to provide an exact measure of these distances and giving us the name parsec, for parallax second of arc, as the basic unit of astronomical distance. With this knowledge, the first link in the chain is secure. A few other stars gathered in groups that are moving rapidly enough for their changing positions in the sky to be measured within a human lifetime can also be set at well-established distances, and in a handful of binary systems whose orbital motions follow Newton's and Kepler's laws (determined from planetary motions in our Solar System), the ratios of the masses of the paired stars can be calculated. If we know the distance to a star, then we know how bright it really is, not just how bright it *seems* to us. If we know the mass of stars for which we know the distance, then we can gain some idea of how mass and luminosity are related, and if we have numerous observations of this kind we might hazard a guess at how the spectral appearance of a star—its color —is related to its absolute brightness, and from this we can determine its probable distance from us by means of its apparent brightness as seen from Earth. This is rather like measuring the brightness of a white-hot poker at a distance of several hundred yards and determining its exact distance by calculations of exactly how hot it is based on measurements of the spectrum it radiates— not an ideal situation by any means. Thus, the second link in the distance-measuring chain is less than perfect. However, as long as some guide to stellar distances can be determined, and as long as the range covered by the measurements is pushed outward into the Milky Way with estimates of the distances of more and more stars, astronomers do gather more and more statistical information. The key evidence that has emerged from such studies of many stars is the knowledge that there is a group of variable stars called the Cepheid variables which fluctuate in brightness in a regular way that seems to produce a period the length of which depends on the mass and luminosity of the particular star (mass and luminosity are related: a more massive star must be hotter from generating more energy to stop it from collapsing under its own gravity). Once the distances to enough Cepheids were measured and the luminosity/ period relation was determined, the distance to any other Cepheid could be determined, in principle, simply by measuring its average apparent luminosity and its period of fluctuation. This enabled the American Edwin Hubble to forge the most important link in the chain of cosmological distances, measuring distances to extragalactic nebulae. In the nearer of these, which are galaxies in their own right, such as the great Andromeda galaxy, individual Cepheids can be detected by their variability and characteristic spectra. The distance to such an external galaxy is so great that, for all practical purposes, all of these Cepheids are at the same distance from us. By averaging the distances to the Cepheids indicated by their luminosity/period, Hubble made the first measurements of the distances to other galaxies.

Though this sounds good, there are problems even at this early stage of cosmological measurement and, by any universal yardstick, these measured galaxies are still very local. Averaging out the distances indicated by measurements of several Cepheids removes any small fluctuations due to slight differences in the luminosity/period relation from one star to another in the external galaxy, but such fluctuations occur (the law is not an exact one) and they affect our understanding of the distances because of their effect closer to home. With only relatively few Cepheids studied in the Milky Way system, astronomers in the twenties were using a luminosity/period relation strongly dependent on the exact properties of just a few stars. Since then, the study of more Cepheids has enabled us to refine the luminosity/period relation and further research has changed the accepted value significantly since Hubble made his first calculations. Probably the value now accepted is close to the true value, if one true value exists, and there is unlikely to be much revision of the scale of universal distance. But it should be remembered that this link depends on the assumption that there is a unique luminosity/period relation for those Cepheids used in the calculation, both here and in other galaxies, and on the further assumption that Cepheids everywhere in the Universe obey the same luminosity/period law. Those are reasonable assumptions, but the use of Cepheids as distance indicators depends only on powerful circumstantial evidence, not on direct measurement.

Red Shifts and Motion

Even while he was opening up the Universe to observation and proving that the Milky Way is but a quiet backwater of the cosmos, Hubble realized this first step was a small one on a long road. Cepheids can be used as distance indicators out to about 10 million light-years, or 3 million parsecs, roughly 100 times the diameter of our Galaxy. It is just as well that galaxies are, relatively speaking, closer together than the stars within galaxies, for a distance measurement which worked only to about 100 times the diameter of the Sun would give a range of observation of just under 9 light-minutes, about 140 million kilometers, which is just 10 million kilometers less than the distance from the Earth to the Sun. If the range of our fundamental techniques of measuring distance were 100 solar diameters, we would not even know the distance to the Sun, much less the distances to other stars. Hubble's first attempt to push measures of the distances of galaxies beyond the 3 Megaparsec Cepheid barrier was based on an assumption that all galaxies have the same absolute brightness, making their apparent brightness (or dimness) a direct indication of their distance. This was an assumption born of desperation, and its consideration by a leading astronomer and cosmologist such as Hubble betrayed a need for desperate remedies in desperate situations. However, it provided a crude

guide to distances which allowed certain specific features
of galaxies, which depend on knowledge of their distances, to emerge, and it gave the first clues from which
Hubble formulated his famous red shift/distance relation, the basic tool of observational cosmologists for the
past fifty years.

The measurements of red shifts in the spectra of astronomical objects and the interpretation of these measurements has become the cornerstone of cosmology and a
happy playground for speculators with bizarre and/or
unfashionable theories. As we have already seen, if the
gravitational field is strong enough, gravity can produce a
red shift. In the twenties, however, and for some time
afterward, the discovery of a shift of spectral lines toward
the red in the spectrum of any astronomical object led
to the natural assumption that the object is moving away
from us. The Doppler effect would produce a red shift
as the receding movement stretched the wave length
of electromagnetic radiation from the object. Similarly,
motion toward us would produce a blue shift, from a
compressed wave length, and indeed this is what we
see in the light of Andromeda, the large galaxy nearest
to our own. In a universe that is, on the average, static,
we would expect to see some small blue shifts and some
small red shifts produced by the random motions of
galaxies. Yet we observe only red shifts, except in the
case of our companion galaxies which form a local group
bound in a gravitational embrace so that their individual
motions are no more typical of the universal situation
than the movement of the Earth around the Sun is
typical of the overall motions of material inside our
Galaxy. Hubble's discovery of the universality of red

shifts (for the galaxies outside the local group) removed the blinkers from the imaginations of cosmologists who had been dealing only with the concept of a static universe. By confirming a prediction within the equations of relativity, this revelation opened the way for those equations to become the accepted means of describing the real Universe. In such a relativistic expanding universe, the red shift will be directly proportional to the distance of a galaxy from us; in the real Universe we must make some allowance for local variations, so it makes more sense to say that the average red shift of a group of galaxies—the average velocity of recession of the whole group—is directly proportional to the group's distance. As long as we deal only with galaxies and clusters of galaxies, there is little room to doubt this interpretation. The light from a distant galaxy is simply the overall product of light from a collection of stars, and as we can study individual stars in detail in our own Galaxy, we can be reasonably sure that light from another galaxy has much the same origin as light from our own Galaxy and its companions. There are ways of achieving similar effects by tinkering with the laws of physics, but the only workable way to do the tinkering produces a situation which is, by definition, indistinguishable from a relativistic expanding universe. We can accept that red shifts within the spectra of galaxies are produced by Doppler motions in the expanding Universe, especially with the independent evidence of expansion supplied by the mute evidence of the dark night sky. But what, exactly, is the proportional constant that relates red shift and distance? How do we know how fast the Universe is expanding?

Measuring Distance

That is a tricky question. It can be answered only by measurements of both distances and red shifts for nearby galaxies. As the red shift/distance relation does not apply to the nearest galaxies of all, those in the local group, we are forced to base our estimates of the most fundamental number in observational cosmology—the Hubble constant of the red shift/distance relation—on measurements that stretch to the limit our conventional yardstick for galaxy distances. This is far from satisfactory, and the Hubble constant is still not well known. There are, however, various tricks that can be used to push our distance estimates out. Hubble's assumption that all galaxies are equally bright is poor. A better guess is that each brightest galaxy in each cluster will be of the same brightness, assuming that there is a limit to how bright any galaxy can be. An alternative to this is the guess that all of the second brightest galaxies have the same absolute brightness—again, the guesses get better as more clusters of galaxies are studied. The determination of the Hubble constant is a problem even for galaxies. When I first studied cosmology in the mid-sixties, it seemed reasonable to use a value of Hubble's constant of 100 kilometers per second velocity of recession for each Megaparsec of distance—even 110 km s^{-1} Mpc^{-1} did not look ridiculous in the light of then current knowledge. Now, only a decade later, 50 km s^{-1} Mpc^{-1} is a more widely accepted figure. In ten years our best guess of the constant has been halved, with the result that the best guess about the distance of every

galaxy has doubled. It's as if we had revised our estimate
of the distance between the Sun and the Earth from
something equivalent to the radius of Venus' orbit to
the equivalent of the radius of Mars' orbit. Our present
understanding of the Universe, even when we are dealing
with galaxies, allows us to describe only the broad sweep
of events, not the detail. Like it or not, cosmology is still
mostly a qualitative, not a quantitative, science.

This qualitative study tells us that clusters of galaxies
recede from the local group and that the farther away
a cluster is, the faster it recedes. In any direction we look
the picture is the same, just as background radiation comes
equally from all directions in space. This does not mean
that our local group marks the center of the Universe.
In a large enough crowd everyone will see a uniform sea
of people stretching away in all directions, even though a
crowd has a center and a perimeter. However, spread out
the crowd to encompass the globe and there will be no
center and no perimeter, which would be analogous to
our Universe except for two basic differences: first, the
Universe fills three dimensions of space, not two; second,
the Universe expands. Mathematically there is no problem in imagining a three-dimensional equivalent to the
closed two-dimensional surface of a sphere. Such a finite
but unbounded three-dimensional universe is merely a
logical progression from the finite but unbounded universes of a circle (a one-dimensional line bent in a
second dimension) and a sphere (a two-dimensional
surface bent round a third dimension). There is the
implication that the three-dimensional universe must
be bent through a fourth dimension, but why not? In
principle we could even measure the curvature of the
Universe to test the idea, and some investigations of the

distances of remote cosmological objects may eventually do just that. Our other options are to argue that the Universe has a perimeter—that it is bounded—but that the edge is so far away that we do not see it, or to accept that the Universe is infinite, which conjures up the image (still mathematically acceptable) of an infinitely large universe getting still bigger as it continually expands. The finite but unbounded universe, analogous to the surface of a sphere, seems the best bet—it also provides the best guide to where we have come from and where we are going.

The universal expansion can be understood more simply. If a shoulder-to-shoulder crowd stood on the surface of an expanding balloon rather than on a solid planet, they would see their neighbors recede from each other with a velocity proportionate to their distance—if each meter of the balloon fabric expanded to two meters, then someone initially two meters away would move out to four meters, and so on. This is the simplest analogy to the red-shift evidence. We live in the three-dimensional equivalent to the surface of an inflating balloon—an expanding hypersphere.

The Quasar Problem

This curious picture has drawn from science fiction a speculation by two writers that is particularly interesting in this connection, though it is based on an incorrect interpretation. It appeared under the headline "science fact," in *Analog,* a magazine specializing in science fiction but generally including some nonfiction articles. This article is worth a close look in spite of its glaring error, because it was published in January 1965, a year before the discovery of the cosmic background radiation as the product of the Big Bang. The writers were concerned about the prospect of viewing the Big Bang directly from its remnant electromagnetic radiation. In one respect William E. Dawson and Ben Bova, the authors of the piece,[2] had more imagination than most of the cosmologists of the time and their article is also interesting because it attempted to explain the very large red shifts found in the spectra of another class of astronomical objects: quasars.

Quasars—objects which appear on a simple photographic plate as ordinary stars but which show a red shift indicating great distance, hence the name quasistellar—provided the first big puzzle in the astronomy that was being made possible by the new techniques of radio, X-ray, and other observations outside the old traditional *visible* part of the electromagnetic spectrum. Throughout the early and middle sixties, the quasar enigma had provided astronomers with food for thought and newspapers with headlines. Then the dramatic discoveries and speculations about pulsars and black holes followed hot on the heels of one another, ousting the quasars from the popular mind and from the minds of many astronomers as well. But the problem of quasars did not go away with inattention. These enigmatic objects are still with us and further observations have only further muddied the speculative waters. Usually, the questions asked by astronomy outnumber the available theoretical answers, but those answers do at least indicate that the right questions are being asked. Such is not the case with quasars, however. Answers proliferate in response to questions about their nature and origin. Facing the curious situation of having more answers than questions, the only convincing explanation is that we must be asking the wrong questions, that a radical rethinking of our understanding of the Universe is needed and, to a large extent, that is the theme of this book. Before setting up any new theories for target practice by other cosmologists and by science-fiction writers, let's examine the alternatives already offered and the reasons none of them is entirely satisfactory.

Quasars are a puzzle because they look like stars but have red shifts like galaxies. They were first identified because of the powerful radio noise many of them emit, but those emissions are coincidental—many radio-quiet quasars are now known. According to the cosmological interpretation of red shifts, and applying Hubble's law to determine their distances, many quasars must be at about the same distances as known galaxies, which is difficult enough for something that looks like a star, but many more have such large red shifts that they must be vastly further away than any observed galaxy. The amount of energy needed for an object to be detectable at such enormous distances is far greater than required in nuclear reactions, which seems to mean that gravity is somehow at work. This is the origin of the Dawson-Bova science-fact–science-fiction idea. In essence, their argument was that if we have a closed universe of the kind previously outlined, then light from other objects in the Universe could reach telescopes on Earth by several routes, equivalent to the great circle routes on the globe. Any one galaxy might be seen from several directions; furthermore, the light from a galaxy might pass us by, orbit around the hypersphere again, be detected on the second trip, and then be interpreted as light from another, much more distant, object. By extrapolation, a succession of fainter and fainter ghost images at greater and greater red shifts is possible, an entertaining theory but not consistent with the observed distribution and spectra of galaxies in the real Universe.

Out to solve the riddle of quasars, Dawson and Bova asked what the ultimately distant view in such a small, closed universe would be. Remember, because light travels at a finite speed, the picture we see of distant objects—at large red shifts—is an old one, a view of the Universe as it used to be. In Dawson's and Bova's model, it seemed natural to posit that at the largest red shifts we would be looking so far back in time that we would see the Big Bang itself, viewed at different times and in different directions, like the multiple images in a hall of mirrors. Quasars, they said, might be just multiple images of the Big Bang. This idea deserves full merit for imagination even though it begs the question of the nature of those quasars with red shifts comparable to the red shifts of ordinary galaxies. There is, however, a fundamental flaw in the argument which serves to explain why we "see" the Big Bang as a flicker of radiation at 2.7 K and not as a multitude of glowing points of light.

Like others before them, Dawson and Bova interpreted the Big Bang to mean that the material and radiation of the Universe burst forth from a highly compressed state into the waiting void of empty space. Going back to the global analogy, a situation similar to this image of creation can be found in the beginning of the present phase of continental drift which followed the breakup of the supercontinent of Pangea in which all of the land surface of the Earth once was concentrated. Spreading out from one place, the continents are now halfway to encompassing the globe; similarly, in a universe of matter gushing forth from one region in a hypersphere, filling the void would take some time, although less would be required for radiation, moving at the speed of light, to whiz around the globe and be detected by our radio telescopes. Unfortunately for this neat picture, the origin, creation, or beginning of the Universe in a Big Bang was not a mighty explosion at some definite place in the pre-existing void. *The void itself was created in the Big Bang.* And the void has always been full of radiation, radiation which has been red shifted (or stretched) as it has expanded with the expanding void. Whatever the nature of the Big Bang, there is no way to view the primordial cosmic gusher except from the inside, as inhabitants. The Big Bang envisaged by Dawson and Bova a decade ago could only have been viewed from outside the Universe, just as a view of the globe as a whole can only be seen from an orbiting spacecraft. Unlike continental drift, the expansion of the Universe is not a movement only of matter; it is also a stretching of the fabric of space, the skin of the balloon. Cosmologically, space has many properties, the stretchability being nothing remarkable as matter can even be viewed as a minor ripple in the fabric of space. The mathematician constructing multidimensional spaces in his imagination through which to imagine the folding of our hyperspherical universe can allow for the possibility of multidimensional outside observers of the phenomenon of our expanding Universe. Such would correspond closely to the idea of a God or gods, bringing forth the questions that if our Universe is inside something greater, what is the greater something still in which the something greater exists, and who are the gods of the gods? However, cosmology is the study of the Universe in which we live and speculation of that sort is beyond its scope. For me, three dimensions of space in which to move about, a fourth in which to fold the hypersphere, and a fifth in the form of time are plenty to work with.

If quasars are not a multiple-image view of the Big Bang, then what are they?

The conventional cosmological explanation of quasars has been built from the interpretation of their red shifts as straightforward Doppler effects produced by the expansion of the Universe in accordance with Hubble's law. A few quasars are now known to have red shifts which indicate velocities almost as great as the speed of light, and, if this interpretation is correct, these remarkable objects are being "seen" as they were only a short time after the Big Bang. If quasars are cosmological, they are the best probes yet available for the study of what the Universe was like long ago. But there are problems. The further away any quasar is, the more energy it must be radiating if it is to be as bright as it seems to our telescopes; how can as much energy as that from a large galaxy be radiated from a very compact source to make quasars visible?

Quasars and the Family of Galaxies

In order to find a way around this energy problem, from the earliest days of the investigation of quasars some theorists have argued that they are not cosmological at all but only what, on photographs of the sky, they seem to be: blue stars in or near our Galaxy. However, that explanation leaves the problem of the red shifts. If quasars are local, it seems to follow that they must have been shot out from the center of our Galaxy in some vast explosion that has sent these blue stars hurtling away at speeds of up to 90 percent of that of light; but that doesn't solve the energy problem. Where did the energy for this supposed vast explosion come from? The third solution to the quasar riddle involves gravitational red shifts: perhaps quasars are compact objects shot out from our Galaxy in a lesser explosion (or series of explosions) and are actually moving slowly, but with a pronounced red shift in their spectra because of their strong gravitational fields. Or, perhaps they *are* cosmological in the sense that they have no links with our Galaxy but are nevertheless massive and compact enough for gravitational effects to contribute at least part of the red shift.

We can see the evidence of more answers than questions—and these were just the first ideas bandied about in the sixties when quasars were discovered. Today there are several more exotic variations on the quasar red-shift theme, but the most disturbing factor about quasars is as clear as it was ten years ago: any hint that the red shifts of these objects are not produced solely by the expansion of the Universe in line with Hubble's law must create suspicion that the red shifts of the galaxies (or at least some galaxies) may have a noncosmological component. Without a satisfactory explanation of why quasars should be different from galaxies, the whole foundation of modern observational cosmology appears shaky. If quasars are not local objects related to our Galaxy (or to the local group of galaxies), then part of their red shift must be cosmological. If part of a red shift is cosmological and part is not, the whole situation becomes rather messy, and this, more than any other reason, seems to be the motivation behind some of the attempts to explain quasars entirely in local terms, for if the beasts are entirely local we can still apply Hubble's law to the red shifts of extragalactic objects.

Just how little can be proved about the state of quasars was highlighted late in 1975 when Dr. Y. P. Varshni of the University of Ottawa published a theory of quasar red shifts that owes nothing either to the Doppler effect or to the gravitational red shift. Varshni's argument begins with the evidence that the same elements are present in quasars and in much the same proportions as the elements detected in the spectral lines of ordinary stars; by happenstance, the lines are merely shifted to the red. So, Varshni argues, it seems likely that quasars are like ordinary stars but that something odd happens to the light from them as it struggles clear of their atmospheres. The something odd he has in mind is a stimulated emission mechanism for the production of radiation at certain frequencies, which could be produced in a star with a violently active atmosphere shooting out hot plasma material. And if the red shift/distance relation breaks down, the energy involved is, by stellar standards, not surprising, since these objects could be in our own cosmic backyard, the Milky Way.

However, it is hard to accept this at face value. There is little experimental evidence to show what kind of spectral lines might be produced by this odd laser effect, and only a small proportion of observed quasars agrees with Varshni's model as it stands. There is so much variation among quasars that almost any theory can be made to fit a few of them, but as yet no theory explains them all.

The value of Varshni's theory is that it demonstrates how bizarre a theory can be and still fit some of the observations, thus making us think again about earlier theories which, though they have become widely accepted, are founded on scarcely more solid ground.

The local/cosmological origin problem received a lot of attention in 1975 when Dr. James Terrell of the Los Alamos Scientific Laboratory offered his explanation of some peculiar blue, starlike objects seen near the powerful radio galaxy Centaurus A. Galaxies emitting powerful radiation at radio frequencies provide an energy puzzle almost as great as the one posed by quasars and, as we shall see, the two may be related.

Often the radio noise from these galaxies is associated with two lobes on opposite sides of the bright optical galaxy, which suggests that some explosive outburst has occurred that ejected fast-moving charged particles which produce radio emissions as they interact with the galaxy's magnetic field. The latest photographs taken through the giant four-meter telescope at Cerro Tololo show that in one of the radio lobes of Centaurus A there are filaments extending away from the galactic center and blue, starlike images of a kind never before seen associated with a galaxy. As Terrell has pointed out, such blue, starlike objects might well have been called quasistellar had not the name already been taken; and, as he has also said, this name may well be the right one.

The concentration of these blue, starlike objects in the Centaurus A radio lobe is about eighty thousand light-years from the center of that galaxy. An observer on a planet circling a star in the galaxy would see faint blue stars. If they were shot out from the nucleus of Centaurus A, they must be moving with a high velocity that would produce a pronounced Doppler red shift to observers in the galaxy. If Terrell's theory is right, these objects must be moving outward from their parent galaxy so fast that even from our own Galaxy the motion should be detectable when photographs we take of them now are compared with those that will be taken in twenty years from now. Terrell's theory at least has the merit that it can, with a little patience, be tested.

Any theory based on but a few observations is difficult to fit into the context of overall quasar observations. There is certainly as much need for an explanation of the energy necessary to power the radio source Centaurus A and to throw out stars at relativistic velocities as there is to explain any quasar within the conventional cosmological picture. And why do we not see any blue-shifted quasars that have been shot out from nearby galaxies and are moving toward us at high speed? Why are the quasars uniformly distributed around the sky while the Centaurus A blue objects are concentrated in one region? Certainly, something in Centaurus A has been detected which needs further investigation. The messy prospect that there may be two kinds of blue stellar objects with high red shift (quasars and quasi-quasars?) cannot be ruled out, disturbing though the prospect may be. It is possible we are making a mistake in lumping all the objects we call quasars together, trying to explain them by one theory. At any rate, the theory that some quasars, at least, are at a cosmological distance and are associated with the nuclei of galaxies gained considerable strength from the discussions of 1975.

One accepted branch of the quasar family is the group of blue starlike objects named after their archetype, BL Lacertae. Seemingly quasars, these have no spectral lines, so their red shifts cannot be measured. They have been investigated by taking long-exposure photographs with powerful telescopes, and often they have been shown surrounded by faint wisps or nebulosities, suggesting that they may be simply the flared-up central regions of galaxies in an unusually bright stage. On the other hand, some BL Lacertae objects which do not seem to have surrounding galaxies lie quite close to other galaxies; it has been argued that these are related in some way to those galaxies, perhaps having been shot out from them like the blue objects near Centaurus A. This is a tricky matter to resolve. Although two objects may appear close together as seen against the sky, they may be at quite different distances along the line of sight and therefore be totally unrelated. Even so, that kind of association has been claimed for many quasar-galaxy pairs. It has been suggested that other quasars are merely very bright nuclei of galaxies, which render it impossible to view the surrounding stars in the way a powerful searchlight would obliterate the light of a candle—or a hundred candles—alongside it.

These lines of evidence and associated observations all point to one set of conclusions: BL Lacertae objects and quasars form part of the same family, and galaxies are also part of that family. BL Lacertae objects have no measured red shifts and as a result astronomers have not been inhibited about associating them with galaxies that lie close to them in the sky; but when a quasar is associated in a similar manner with a galaxy, the two almost invariably have different red shifts, which—using

Hubble's law—places them at different distances from us. From this we conclude, finally, that the red shift is not produced uniquely by the expansion of the Universe, at least where quasars are concerned, but Hubble's law remains the best explanation of the red shifts of quiet galaxies having no obvious activity and no quasarlike features.

This view is not held by the entire astronomical community; indeed, where quasars are concerned it is impossible to find any one view that represents the established theory. Professor Geoffrey Burbidge has summed it up:

> I believe that you have to look at the evidence and counterevidence or counterarguments very carefully . . . it's like trying to get to the top of a tree when you are blindfolded. You go up the trunk and find two branches. You take either the left or the right and climb it. It forks again and eventually you reach the top of the tree or somewhere in the tree. What is the probability that you got to the top in the most direct way, or even got there at all? At every turn you have made a decision. At any point you may have made the wrong decision. *I believe somewhere in this subject we may already have made the wrong decision.*[3] [Italics mine.]

In my view, that wrong turning came through too long adherence to the sacrosanct interpretation of all red shifts according to Hubble. Hubble's law is one of the most dramatic and powerful tools of cosmology *when applied to the study of galaxies.* But there is no basis for the assumption that all of the red shift in every quasar arises in the same way. No one has found a Cepheid variable inside a quasar in order to measure its distance directly. Even abandoning the dogma of cosmological red shifts for quasars, we have problems enough to explain their energy production and the energy production of radio and other violently active galaxies. Nonetheless, quasars now can be related to the galaxy family, both categorically and, in many cases, physically.

Quasars and White Holes

Leaving aside the red-shift evidence for the time being, quasars can be divided, by means of their luminosity, into two categories. Some have the same sort of luminosity as bright galaxies in the same cluster. These lie in the same direction as clusters of galaxies and it seems natural to accept them as members of those clusters, which also gives us an idea of their distances when we measure red shifts of the galaxies in the clusters. The energy they produce is not remarkable, but the fact that the energy comes from a very compact source, the size of the nucleus of a galaxy, is. Quasars in the second category—those identified as being physically related to specific galaxies, perhaps ejected from them—are always found to be much fainter than their companions, about one-hundredth as bright as the associated galaxy. Of course, to be even one-hundredth as bright as a galaxy while occupying only a fraction of the volume of a galaxy is a considerable feat, and these fainter quasars are spectacular producers of energy from extremely compact sources. From this evidence, Dr. T. Jaakkola and his colleagues in Helsinki have made a bold leap by suggesting that the two kinds of quasars actually could evolve into galaxies, the brighter kind becoming giant galaxies and the dimmer quasars evolving into dwarf galaxies. This could be achieved by expansion of material out of the compact quasar state.

What sort of object is highly energetic, is powered by gravitation, and expands outward from a compact state to produce a cloud of material? It is a cosmic gusher, or a white hole! Simply by rejecting the conventional cosmological interpretation of quasar red shifts, all this —the link between quasars and galaxies, the resolution of the energy problem, and perhaps a clue to the origin of our own Galaxy as the offspring of a quasar—has come. The gains certainly seem to outweigh the losses. Before developing this idea in detail to show how we may be the product of an outwardly gushing quasar—a galactic gusher—and relating the creation of galaxies in such gushers to the creation of the Universe in the original cosmic gusher, one ghost should first be laid— that of the black hole.

The idea that quasars might represent the death throes of galaxies seems to have been around for as long as the idea that they might mark the birth pangs of galaxies. The speculation that, as galaxies age more and more, their stars evolve into small black holes and that the nucleus of an aging galaxy might become a large and growing black hole, has gone hand in hand with this idea. Such a black hole could gobble up matter remaining in the galaxy and produce a large amount of radiation as some of the mass–energy of the matter was released when, through the repeated collisions of particles spiraling into the mouth of the black hole, it heated up. It has even been suggested that a black hole might be growing at the center of our own Galaxy. The possibility cannot be ruled out, and such a process might exist even if it had nothing to do with quasars. But does the concept of quasars as black holes, or as dying galaxies, stand up in the face of the evidence? Even if only part of the red shift in the light from a quasar is cosmological, these objects are as distant from us as galaxies, and that means we see them as they were when the Universe was younger. Does it then make sense to explain energetic events *early* in the history of the Universe as being caused by the *death* of galaxies? The problem posed by the early Universe is where galaxies came from, not where they are going! In any case, assuming an expanding Universe, itself the product of a cosmic gusher, can we jump to the conclusion that *any* energetic process is associated with a black hole? We have no unequivocal, direct evidence that black holes exist (although the circumstantial evidence is strong, and I believe it), but we do know for certain that if our cosmological ideas are correct there is at least one white hole—the Big Bang— and we are living in its aftermath. Surely, it makes more sense to explain energetic events in terms of the *birth* of galaxies by outward expansion along with the whole universal outward expansion—and that is just what we are now in a position to do.

3
GALACTIC GUSHERS

Astronomers have been faced both with the mystery of the energy process which powers quasars and with the problem of accounting for the profligate way in which radio galaxies and the violently exploding galaxies known as Seyferts blast energy and matter outward. For a long time, it looked as though the puzzle would be further complicated by the need for different explanations for each category of violent object in the Universe. Over the past ten years or so, however, a significant trend has emerged from the observations: the more information we have about galactic-scale violent objects in the Universe, the more they seem to resemble one another. A compact class of galaxies called the N-galaxies can be fitted into the overall picture as being intermediate between quasars and Seyferts; the radio emissions from radio galaxies and from quasars are so similar that there is no method of distinguishing between the two kinds of objects by radio observations alone, which, of course, is why astronomers spend so much time and trouble locating the optical counterparts of cosmic radio sources. There seems to be a continuous gradation in physical characteristics from the most compact energetic sources, the quasars, through compact galaxies, N-galaxies, Seyferts, and peculiar but less energetic galaxies, and on to the quietly respectable so-called normal galaxies.

The Radiating Galaxies

The Seyfert galaxies in particular, which are just about halfway along this chain from quasars to normal galaxies, have been well studied and deserve more than a passing mention. They are named after Carl Seyfert who first identified them as a separate class in 1943. Superficially, the Seyferts resemble normal spiral galaxies like our own in which two arms of bright stars, lined with dark clouds of gas and dust, coil outward from a central nucleus to form a flattened disc. However, the nucleus of a Seyfert galaxy, unlike that of an ordinary spiral, is very bright and is even smaller than usual; it shows strong emission lines in its spectrum, whereas the spectra of ordinary galactic nuclei show only absorption lines. This means that the light is being radiated by high temperature gases concentrated in the central regions. Furthermore, this radiation is subject to rapid variations on irregular time-scales. This can only be a sign of violent activity so extreme that astronomers talk in terms of catastrophic processes at the centers of these galaxies.

Stripped of its surrounding spiral arms, the nucleus of a Seyfert galaxy would be indistinguishable from a quasar. Simply because Seyferts were found first and have always been classed as galaxies (albeit peculiar energetic galaxies), it has been accepted as gospel that red shifts measured for Seyferts strictly obey Hubble's law and are accurate distance indicators. About the Seyfert galaxy 3C 120, which is surrounded by a cloud of very bright small radio sources (seemingly ejected by the parent galaxy), Ludwig Oster writes:

> Since in the case of 3C 120, a spiral galaxy, there is no question that the observed red shift is a distance indicator, we can translate the angular diameter into linear size and obtain for the smallest source [in this cloud] the tiny diameter of about 0.1 parsec.[1]

Of course, if there is any real link between quasars and Seyferts, and if there is any doubt about the use of red shifts as distance indicators for quasars, there must be some doubt about the use of red shifts as distance indicators for Seyferts. This emphasizes a problem which again has been highlighted by Geoffrey Burbidge, who says, "Cosmology is similar to religion in many ways . . . in the sense that in most cases we are talking about a large measure of belief and a rather small amount of information."[2] Another eminent astronomer, John Faulkner, has suggested that perhaps cosmologists should always state the opinions upon which they base their facts. This seems entirely appropriate to anyone who bases "facts" about the size of radio sources associated with

Seyferts on the opinion that "there is no question that the observed red shift is a distance indicator."

A Challenge to Hubble

By discarding preconceived notions about red shifts as indicators of distance, Halton Arp of the Hale Observatories has come up with a picture of the Universe, startlingly different from the establishment view, in which groups of galaxies contain a range of objects, from quasars through compact galaxies and high-red-shift peculiar galaxies as well as the more diffuse normal galaxies supposed to make up the sole population of clusters and groups of galaxies of the establishment picture. Arp's unconventional ideas have not been welcomed by the establishment; indeed, if the astronomical establishment's views can be likened in some ways to religious dogma, then Arp's views have been treated as heresy and thus deemed unworthy of serious examination. For a long time, this was the attitude of all too many people toward Arp's novel approach and toward similar investigations by V. A. Ambartsumian and his colleagues in the USSR. Only in the past few years, appreciating that many features of energetic processes in the Universe cannot, after all, be explained within the framework of accepted dogma, have many astronomers realized that a ready-made, self-consistent alternative view of the Universe has existed for years. The idea of energetic processes associated with discordant red shifts and the ejection of material from quasars and from the nuclei of galaxies has gained in strength over the years as more and more objects have been found which fit this pattern but do not fit the older, established view of the Universe.

Arp's work has been concentrated on finding physical links between galaxies and other objects which have different red shifts. The rationale behind this aim is simple. If two galaxies are physically attached, they must be at about the same distance from us; so their having different red shifts proves that for one of them at least the red shift is not a guide to distance. Arp has now produced photographic evidence for a vast array of such cases. Any one of them might be a coincidence of some kind or a special case, but they cannot all be accidental, and some of the discrepancies between the red shifts of physically linked sources are dramatic in the extreme. Take the Seyfert NGC 7603, which has a red shift corresponding to a recession velocity of 8,800 km a second. It is attached to a small, peculiar galaxy which shows a red shift equivalent to 16,900 kms^{-1}, almost twice as great. There is clear evidence, gathered by Arp, to show that these two galaxies are indeed physically related— the interaction of their separate gravitational fields produces tidal effects which distort the shapes of the two galaxies. This evidence implies that half the red shift of the companion must arise in some way quite unrelated to its motion in the expanding Universe—this example alone suffices to cast doubts on the general applicability of the red-shift/distance relation, indicating the need for a new leap of imagination forward from what has now become, to astronomers at least, the commonsense world view. Could such a compact galaxy actually have been ejected from the larger Seyfert? If so, what would it look like in later epochs as the system evolves? Perhaps we have here a clue to the origin of the huge sources of radio emission now known to exist in the Universe. Systems spread across hundreds of kiloparsecs and associated with galaxies only one-tenth as large are now regarded as nothing unusual; for some sources identified in the early seventies, the region of radio emission seems to be several million parsecs across, more than a hundred times as extensive as a galaxy like our own. Somehow, the energy which feeds these radio sources must be spread over great volumes of space, and how better than by outward explosions of matter from gushing galactic nuclei or quasars? Radio astronomers seem to have come late to this realization, but they have appreciated the idea all the more for having first tried and failed to explain their observations by conventional methods. In 1970, Robert Hjellming of the Green Bank Observatory was so delighted when he first came across the idea of white holes that he wrote to the journal *Nature* and pointed out the possibilities inherent in applying the idea to quasars and energetic galactic nuclei. Yet relativists and some cosmologists had been aware of the concept as an abstract possibility for many years before the radio astronomers discovered its applicability in the real Universe.

Galaxy Cores

If quasars are outwardly gushing white holes, it certainly seems plausible that galaxies might be built up from the pools of matter that have exploded outward into a local region of space. Yet can theory tell us anything about the appearance of such a cosmic gusher in action? According to Professor J. V. Narlikar, who is best known through his collaborations with Fred Hoyle on aspects of the Steady State theory, and his colleagues at the Tata Institute in Bombay, it is indeed possible to calculate the expected spectrum of light from an active white hole, under a variety of different conditions. They find that these gushers could well appear to outside observers to be like the observed range of energetic phenomena in the Universe—a range embracing not only quasars, Seyferts, and other energetic galaxies but even encompassing smaller events such as X-ray-star explosions within our Galaxy. This theory is a long way from gaining acceptance by the astronomical establishment, considering that only recently has it become respectable to talk about white holes as possible features of the real Universe. For the time being, we will work on the assumption that galaxies are the possible products of cosmic gushers. As it happens, there is already a great deal of evidence and a variety of calculations which show (quite independently of theories of cosmic gushers, white holes, quasars, or whatever) that there must be something unusual, in the form of a compact object, at the centers of many, and perhaps all, galaxies.

As well as spiral galaxies like our own, the Universe contains elliptical galaxies, which have a more even distribution of stars and no spiral structure, within an overall configuration ranging from spherical to cigar-shaped. There are irregular galaxies which do not fit either main category; such as the Magellanic Clouds, which are satellites of the Milky Way. For the ellipticals, especially, estimates of mass and brightness of the galaxies lead to a very curious problem. As far as we can tell, the light from these galaxies is only as much as we would expect to see from a collection of average stars with a total mass of only one quarter of the mass of the whole galaxy. Somewhere in the bright ellipticals, however, there is three times as much material as we can see in bright stars, locked up in some invisible aggregate. This is especially odd as the ellipticals, unlike spirals, do not contain large quantities of dust which can be detected where, blotting out the light from underlying stars, it produces dark lanes; this missing mass is very well hidden indeed. One of the first proposals to explain this was that there might be a black hole at the center of every elliptical galaxy (and probably at the center of every spiral as well) and that the visible stars are bound to the nucleus by the gravity of the central black hole. Calculations of the distribution of stars which should arise in such a strong gravitational field provide good support for this idea—but where could the black hole have come from? We are back to the problem of explaining quasars as the deaths of galaxies, and we can solve the problem just as before. What the calculations of missing mass tell us is that there must be a compact object at the center of each galaxy; the interpretation of this to mean black hole is another example of the influence of prejudice at work, which seems especially odd in the face of the other obvious question of where the visible bright stars came from in the first place. The possibility that they were created in the outward expansion of a cosmic gusher, which is now quiet in typical ellipticals but remains active in galaxies such as Seyferts, is not something to dismiss lightly. Perhaps it is correct that such ellipticals do now contain black holes at their centers, but these would be black holes that have formed from the recollapse of white holes following their initial bursts of activity in which the stars of the galaxies were created. Or perhaps the cosmic gushers are not continuous but are subject to bursts of white-hole activity from time to time. Either way, it is quite clear from detailed calculations that stars forming in the debris of a massive cosmic gusher in the expanding Universe will form a distribution just like that of stars we see in elliptical galaxies. That leaves something of a problem over spiral and elliptical galaxies but not too great a difficulty. Ellipticals are the obvious end product of smooth, uniform expansion away from a white hole. More erratic outbursts may produce more bizarre phenomena, and it is also possible that spiral galaxies are formed by the accretion of other material in the Universe onto the central core of an elliptical galaxy, attracted there by the mass of the dense, compact white hole.

One theory suggests that both the violent activity of many objects and the ejection of energetic compact objects from some galactic nuclei may be due to the presence of two or more original compact objects orbiting each other in the parent galaxy's nucleus, a situation which produces occasional ejections of one fragment through the simple, well-understood laws of orbital dynamics. This is a grand and wonderful speculation—not just one but several white holes, orbiting one another at the centers of active galaxies with occasional eruptions and occasional ejections of a complete white hole which can then grow into a new galaxy in its own right! Spectacular though the idea is, it certainly fits in well with the observed fact that galaxies are involved in violent events which eject material across vast intergalactic distances. It is supported by strong indications from the work of Arp and a few others that peculiar, compact galaxies are physically ejected from the centers of larger active galaxies. In the most extreme cases, photographs of groups of galaxies show chains of physically connected galaxies which may have been ejected from one another in successive violent events, but that would require an even grander theory than the idea of several compact objects orbiting at the hearts of Seyferts, quasars, and related objects. Could the white holes actually fragment so that galaxies would reproduce like amoebae, by parthenogenesis? That sounds so unlikely in terms of our everyday experience of the behavior of matter that it's worth looking at the standard theories of galaxy formation to show just how hopeless they are as explanations of the real Universe. Fissioning white holes might seem like a solution of last resort, but when no other theory provides any kind of satisfactory solution, that solution is surely the one we must accept.

Galactic Births

The problem with all the conventional theories of galaxy formation is that they are based on the assumption (the opinion on which the facts are based) that we must begin with a uniform spread of material in the expanding Universe. If you have a nice, even spread of this kind, and if, at the same time, everything is spreading out more and more as the Universe expands, it is very difficult to explain why or how local regions of the uniform expanding gas (mainly hydrogen, with a little helium produced in the Big Bang) can do just the opposite and contract into nice, compact, dense clouds of gas in which stars form to produce galaxies. There is also no mention of where the missing mass of galaxies is hidden, but let's leave that question aside for now; the conventional theories are in enough trouble without it.

If the Universe were static, as everyone believed until half a century ago, there would be no problem in explaining why large uniform clouds of gas should fragment and collapse to form galaxies and stars. Newton himself seems to have been aware of this and commented on the instability of such a self-gravitating medium in a letter to Dr. Bentley. It was not until the twenties that a proper mathematical description of this fragmentation process was produced by James Jeans, ironically just at the time it was becoming clear that the Universe is not at all static. Of course, even in a static universe a proof that uniform clouds of gas collapse to form galaxies begs the question of the origin of the gas in the first place, so the whole idea is on very shaky ground. This seems to have had no inhibiting effect on succeeding generations of astronomers, however, who happily took over Jeans' calculations of the criteria for stability (or instability) of gas clouds in a *static* universe and applied them to the real *expanding* Universe, assuming that the only effect of the expansion is to move the collapsing gas clouds farther away from one another. According to theories based on this idea, the variety of galaxies and clusters of galaxies we see around us is supposed to result from various irregularities in the original cloud of gas. The assumption is that the Universe expands for some time after the Big Bang until a situation is reached where the Jeans criterion can be applied approximately. Such convenient, docile behavior of the Universe to match the opinions of these cosmologists hardly seems plausible to anyone who doesn't share their opinions, but it is worth following some of these theories through to demonstrate how severe the constraints of convention can be.

If the Universe ever did reach a stage where it contained turbulent, giant clouds of gas conveniently separated from one another, then each turbulent cloud could fragment into a cluster of galaxies, with an individual galaxy being the product of each eddy in the turbulent flow of the parent cloud. The theory is then faced with the severe problem of explaining why all galaxies are not spirals, which it does in a rather halfhearted sort of way. The theory suggests that galaxies steadily lose material from their edges, wasting away until only the nuclei are left. Some galaxies, we are asked to believe, have completed this process and look like ellipticals; others of the same size, formed at the same time, have scarcely lost any material, and we see them as spirals. Another problem lies in the fact that, according to this theory, stars should form very rapidly (by astronomical standards), being produced in only about five million years from eddies within the larger eddy of a galaxy. Why, then, is there any leftover material at all? Surely, such an efficient process of star formation should have used up all the spare gas long ago in the history of a galaxy like our own. The answer to this one is, essentially, magic. According to the theory, star formation stopped because the presence of the first generation of stars, in some unexplained way, inhibited further star formation. Given the problems so far, the discovery that the theory can explain neither the formation of binary stars nor the formation of pairs of galaxies seems almost immaterial, even though, according to current ideas, many and perhaps most stars occur in binary pairs or multiple groups. Even when some astronomers tried to salvage something of this theory in the early seventies, the best they could claim was that under favorable conditions it might account for the formation of spiral galaxies, presumably containing no binaries and therefore no supernovae or pulsars. Turbulence in collapsing gas clouds as a primary factor in galaxy formation is a hopeless concept. Surely, there must be better ideas.

Maybe. But not, it seems, if you try to retain gravitational instability as a driving force. It is generally asking too much of any simple theory in astronomy to expect an answer to all the problems, or even to most of them. It does seem, however, that the gravitational instability idea fails to answer the most important questions and cannot explain many special cases. In the early fifties, Hoyle summed up the situation by presenting a model of galaxy formation, based on gravitational instability, which either by accident or by design served mainly to highlight the deficiencies of that kind of model. The theory starts out from "pre-galaxies" in the form of clouds of gas at a density of 10^{-27} gm cm^{-3}. That might seem a low density by our everyday standards—about six atoms of hydrogen in every ten liters of space—but that's about one thousand times the average density of the Universe, if all the material now locked up in stars and galaxies were spread out uniformly, and it is very hard to see how that crucial first step in separating out denser gas clouds could have occurred if the material originally was uniformly spread out. Still, if such clouds could exist they certainly would collapse, becoming hotter as they did so, as gravitational potential energy was converted into the kinetic energy of the motions of the atoms, which means heat. At a temperature of about

25,000 degrees, there would be a phase during which the gravitational energy went not into heating the cloud but into stripping electrons from hydrogen atoms until complete ionization of the cloud material occurred; because of this stripping the clouds would form into two very different kinds: cold, un-ionized clouds and hot, ionized material. As Hoyle presented the theory two decades ago, however, only the cold clouds were dealt with in any detail, and the role of the hot clouds was established as that of a scapegoat for anything which could not be explained by the cold-cloud model, with no detailed explanation of how they might achieve this feat. Although all this speculation and opinion seems less than relevant to the real Universe, the model does become quite relevant when at last it gets down to the fine detail of explaining how stars can form in collapsing gas clouds. We can see such clouds in our Galaxy, and as we know that some stars are being formed right now, so there is every likelihood that a model of how stars form from dense gas clouds could be directly applicable. Unfortunately, there is even a snag here with the original theory because there is nothing to stop the collapsing clouds from fragmenting more and more to produce tiny bits and pieces, with masses appropriate to planets rather than to stars. There are ways round this and some of the other difficulties, and by being patched with ever more complicated improvements, this theory has remained respectable enough for discussion and published papers about it to appear even in the seventies. It is, however, more an exercise in ingenuity for mathematical physicists and astronomers than any real attack on the fundamental problems of the Universe.

The Clustering Model

The failure of the idea of galaxy formation as a process of collapse starting out from large clouds of gas has encouraged work on a theory that starts from the opposite point of view, but still lies within the framework of a Universe filled at some early epoch with a nearly uniform cloud of material. Since the early sixties, Professor David Layzer of Harvard University has been developing a model in which the observed inhomogeneity of the Universe on the scale of galaxies and clusters of galaxies is the product not of a continuing fragmentation process but of an ongoing clustering process. Like water droplets that form in water vapor as it cools below the boiling point, stars, galaxies, and other bodies are explained in this model as the aggregation of smaller particles. The theory in principle provides for the production of a hierarchy of different-sized aggregates, from a comet to stars and galaxies to clusters of galaxies and even superclusters of galaxies. All that is necessary, according to Layzer, is that, at some past epoch, the distribution of matter in the Universe was *nearly* uniform but contained local irregularities of the kind that arise from the random movements of the atoms in the universal cloud. Once a few particles get together to form a group bound by their own gravity, the whole process can be repeated on a larger scale, with each group of particles now acting as a single particle, and so on, up the scale.

This model is still very much alive, at least in the minds of Layzer and his students, and as recently as

December 1975, in an article in *Scientific American*,[3] Layzer described the latest development of the concept. According to this account, about fifteen minutes after the Big Bang the Universe crystallized, or froze, into an alloy of metallic hydrogen and helium, which, as the expansion continued, shattered into fragments of about the mass of a planet. These fragments then formed the gas for the next phase of the growth of fluctuations, so that, according to Layzer, "eventually a hierarchy of structures is formed, corresponding to stars, galaxies, and clusters of galaxies seen today." Apart from the worrying lack of any satisfactory explanation of the cosmic background radiation in this model, there is an obvious flaw which has existed since the earliest days of the clustering theory, which holds that planets form before stars and that stars form before galaxies—rather hard to reconcile with the existence of planets like Earth, since the heavy elements are generally explained as being the product of nuclear-fusion reactions in stars. Furthermore, why should stars still be forming in the Galaxy if Layzer's model is correct? At best, it seems we need another theory of star and planet formation to account for present conditions, even if the clustering idea explains where the Galaxy first came from. On the other hand, any theory that can explain present-day formation of stars and planets can be extended to explain the formation of all the stars and planets, removing the need for the clustering theory. The most fundamental flaw in all of the models based on a uniform distribution of material throughout the Universe shortly after the Big Bang is the time it has taken for irregularities the size of galaxies to grow up. Whether you favor a fragmentation approach or a clustering approach, the same problem is there. It simply takes much longer than about 15,000 million years for galaxy-sized irregularities to develop. This is shown particularly clearly when the Jeans criterion is calculated properly within the framework of an expanding universe. The criterion for fragmentation and collapse of gas clouds still works for the real Universe, but unless the Universe is a great deal older than all the evidence suggests, there has not yet been anywhere near enough time for this kind of fragmentation to have produced the varied structure we see around us. Equivalent calculations produce the same time-scale difficulty for the clustering theories. In essence, either process for producing galaxies and clusters of galaxies in an initially uniform, expanding universe would only work if the Universe is in a steady state, or so much older than our best theories suggest that it would, for all practical purposes, be steady state. Either both concepts of galaxy formation are wrong or all the observational evidence for the Big Bang, including background radiation, has been completely misinterpreted. The conclusion must be that the Universe was not completely homogeneous, even a few minutes after the Big Bang.

The Option of Anticollapse

This realization has led to the beginnings of a new approach to the problem of galaxy formation. Some astronomers have begun to dip into theories allowed by the assumption of some initial lumpiness from which galaxies have grown, but they have not yet taken the plunge of accepting the possibility that the initial lumps may not have been merely seeds on which galaxies grew, but may have contained the mass of complete galaxies locked up in white holes. This theory has been around for as long as the clustering idea, and has existed even longer in a partial form. The mainstream of astronomical thought is slowly shifting toward the idea of cosmic gushers, but it is not there yet. Some calculations made by Michael Ryan of the University of Texas in the early seventies indicate the extremes of daring still permissible within the boundaries of the mainstream. Ryan proceeded from the fact the galaxies could not grow from a uniform distribution of matter in the Universe in the available time; he tried to find out how much initial inhomo-geneity—or lumpiness—would be needed to allow the galaxy formation process to occur quickly enough to fit in with the established time-scale of events since the Big Bang. The answer is that a compact lump of matter equivalent to the mass of ten million suns—which is small compared with the mass of a large galaxy—would produce a strong enough gravitational influence on the surrounding material to act as the nucleus for the growth of a galaxy. It is a sign of the times that Ryan assumes that such a compact massive object would be a black hole, arguing that every galaxy larger than about ten million solar masses must contain a black hole at the center (smaller galaxies would have had time to form even in a universe between 10,000 and 15,000 million years old)—the black-hole assumption is an unwarranted extension of the results of the calculations, made to fit preconceived opinions. The mathematics say that a collapsed concentration of matter must lie at the center of every galaxy bigger than ten million solar masses, but they do not say anything about the state of that matter. Ryan's calculations show that if lesser white holes can exist within the framework of the greater white hole of the expanding Universe, objects very much like galaxies would form around them even before they began their own gushing outbursts. While they remained quiet, such retarded cores would have no effect other than their attractive gravitational influence on the surrounding material, perhaps allowing the growth of galaxies, in some cases, as suggested by Ryan. During an outburst from its collapsed state of a retarded core, we might well see something very like a Seyfert galaxy—the central cosmic gusher would burst forth from behind the veil of stars which had formed near it over the past millions of years. The differences between Seyferts, N-galaxies, quasars, ordinary galaxies, and the rest then become simply ones of degree. The size of the retarded core—the potential cosmic gusher—determines the size and shape of the surrounding protogalaxy. The intensity of cosmic gusher outbursts is obviously an important factor and may itself depend on the mass available to gush. The two big unanswered questions about this model are why they should gush at all (or, rather, why the outburst is delayed) and whether retarded cores can gush more than once, in repeated outbursts. The answers seem to be inextricably linked to the fundamental question of why the Universe itself exists and how it began to gush; the questions cannot satisfactorily be answered within the framework of our present knowledge of the laws of physics any more than the question of the ultimate cause of the origin of the Universe can be answered. These questions point to the necessary development of physics and cosmology beyond the limits of relativity theory in the same way that the existence of the Universe and its creation in a Big Bang points to the need for a theoretical development beyond that of relativity. Apart from that, the nature of such cosmic gushers is exactly in line with our observations of the real Universe.

This is most simply demonstrated by the oldest trick in the cosmologist's book: to imagine the Universe to be running in the opposite direction, like a reversed film, so that galaxies and clusters of galaxies move together as the Universe contracts toward the initial singularity. This situation is analogous to the collapse of the Universe into a black-hole singularity, and it produces a reflection of this in the behavior of local regions. We know that some regions of the Universe are more dense than others; imagine sitting in a region of average density watching a denser galaxy or cluster participating in this mythical universal collapse. With everything shrinking and densities increasing, a time must come when the densest local regions reach the critical density for black-hole formation and disappear behind their respective event horizons; the lights go out as the Universe shrinks and becomes more dense until it forms a compact collection of black holes with some intermediate material. Our imagination then breaks down, along with the known laws of physics, as these lesser singularities merge into the greater singularity of the universal black hole.

But the Universe is not collapsing—it is expanding. It is a white hole, not black. In that case, regions of relatively large density, lesser singularities within the overall singularity of the creation of the Universe, follow the expansion as lesser white holes. In an expanding universe, it is natural to look to the expansion of cosmic gushers as a physical explanation for the presence of irregularities such as galaxies. The association of irregularities with black holes is natural only in a collapsing universe, the time-reversal of our real surroundings. In spite of its unnatural appearance compared with everyday events here on Earth, the cosmic gusher concept is best for explaining the presence of galaxies in the real Universe. It is our everyday ideas, gained from experience on one small planet orbiting an insignificant star in a rather ordinary galaxy, that fail when applied to greater things. And whereas the attempt to generalize from the particular case of our own planet, Sun, and Galaxy has proved a hopeless failure, the general idea of cosmic gushers can be applied with great success to explain the present situation within our Galaxy and here on Earth itself. The idea also raises a prospect far more awesome than any black hole: is it possible that our Galaxy may one day become a quasar as the central retarded core switches into its cosmic gusher phase? And if so, what would be the effect on life on Earth—or in the whole Galaxy?

Part II
Where Are We Now?

4

OUR MILKY WAY GALAXY

As the idea that the center of our Galaxy might explode with the violence of a bright quasar has obvious doomsday story possibilities, it has been picked up by science-fiction writers and has appeared several times. Larry Niven uses an explosion of the galactic core as background to many of his stories of the future, and in *Ringworld* he has whole civilizations fleeing from our Galaxy to escape the ensuing holocaust. Such an evacuation would require, of course, some foreknowledge of the event, and if no signal can travel faster than light, there would be no way of finding out about the explosion until its effects arrived.[1]

The only way we will know if our Galaxy turns into a quasar will be when the blast of light, the electromagnetic radiation, and the high-energy particles reach us. Since we orbit the Galaxy at a distance of about ten kiloparsecs from the nucleus, for all we know the nucleus could have exploded any time in the past 30,000 years without our yet knowing about it. The light from the explosion, closely followed by a sleet of energetic cosmic-ray particles, which would take that long to reach us, may even now be on its way—just the situation at the beginning of Fred and Geoffrey Hoyle's *The Inferno*. As the story unfolds, the blast from the quasar at the center of the Galaxy reaches the Earth and destroys civilization. It is not surprising that, with Fred Hoyle involved, the calculations of energies and the implications for our small planet are completely sound, although the chance of our Galaxy exploding in the near future is next to nil. *The Inferno* is an excellent source for facts about the energy involved in quasar explosions and what this means in practical terms even at a distance of ten kiloparsecs. The story may be only a good yarn for us, but, when you read it, remember that what the Hoyles describe may represent events that meant disaster to other civilizations inhabiting planets which circle stars only a few kiloparsecs from those explosions. A black hole can only sit and wait for you to pass unwittingly close before doing you harm, but a white hole can explode outward across the light-years to destroy whole galaxies of people. Equally, however, such explosions, in all probability, were responsible for the creation of the Galaxy as we know it and for the existence of our civilization. One might say that the white hole giveth, the white hole taketh away.

The central regions of our Galaxy, like the central regions of other spirals, are like elliptical galaxies. Elliptical galaxies come in all sizes, and some of the

globular clusters of stars associated with our Galaxy are essentially the same as small, spherical galaxies of the elliptical type. Surrounding the Galaxy and stretching out through a spherical volume of space, these globular clusters contain the oldest stars of the Galaxy. Their formation was clearly related to the formation of the first component of our Galaxy, the central nucleus or elliptical component. The stars of the disc that surround this elliptical center and those of the spiral arms are younger, later additions to the basic elliptical structure. It may be that all galaxies, having initially formed as ellipticals under the gravitational influence of the central retarded core, have the potential to grow into spirals through the quasar-Seyfert process, with extra material pouring from the center and later settling into the disc. Perhaps this behavior can occur only for a certain fraction of the initially retarded cores, satisfying some special conditions. Either way, that seems to be what has produced the diverse objects of the Milky Way, including our Solar System and ourselves.

Globular Clusters

Bright globular clusters do not enter into this evolutionary story directly; formed at the earliest stage of the development of our Galaxy, they have been bystanders to the later, more dramatic events. Yet they deserve mention, since these concentrations of stars are on the grand scale by comparison with our immediate stellar neighborhood, and, also, because their presence may be related to the existence of collapsed objects on a smaller scale than that of the retarded core at the galactic center.

The great cluster in the constellation Hercules seems typical and is so bright that even at a distance of 30,000 light-years (roughly the same as the distance to the galactic center, but in a different direction) astronomers have been able to make a thorough study of the overall properties of the tens of thousands of stars which make up the cluster. The distance measurement comes from studies of Cepheid variables within the cluster, and the study of such objects is akin to the study of miniature elliptical galaxies. Some of the clusters are even slightly elliptical, being elongated in one direction by 10 to 15 percent, and, although this could be the result of collisional disturbances in the past or of rotational effects, it may be that this feature is another similarity between the clusters and real elliptical galaxies. More than a hundred globular clusters are known to be associated with the Milky Way and another hundred or so may exist but are hidden from us by the intervening material of the Milky Way itself. Even so, this is a tiny number compared with the number of stars in the Galaxy—or in a globular cluster—and, clearly, such objects are special, even by galactic standards. According to some estimates, as many as one-third of all globular clusters may be intergalactic, not tied to any parent galaxy at all; only a few such systems have been studied in detail— they are too small to be scrutinized intensively at any great distance—and those seem to be somewhat larger in diameter than galactic globular clusters, with a thinner density of stars throughout their larger volume.

The conventional view of the formation of globular clusters is that they were produced by the collapse and fragmentation of self-gravitating volumes of gas during the collapse of the greater region of self-gravitating gas that became our Galaxy. Doubts about the validity of this idea of galaxy formation naturally extend to doubts about its validity for the formation of globular clusters; however, if a retarded core at the center of the Galaxy has restrained the expansion of the universal gas locally, it becomes quite feasible to account for the formation of systems like globular clusters by local gravitational concentrations of material within the restrained cloud. On the other hand, should you wish to keep to a more tidy model in which globular clusters grow on mini-retarded cores, or even on black holes, which are themselves satellites of the central collapsed object in the galactic nucleus, a case could be made to support that theory.

The same equations apply on a smaller scale. Stars forming in the cloud of material restrained by a small retarded core would have a spherical or slightly elliptical distribution, with a very bright central region, as seen in globular clusters. Several X-ray sources have now been identified with globular clusters, and this has encouraged speculation that there may be massive black holes at their centers. As ever, the same evidence applies to the existence of retarded cores or white holes—it is just that it is more fashionable these days to include black holes in the title of a scientific paper. Perhaps the idea is correct—except that the black hole may have originated in the Big Bang, not through later collapse. Globular clusters, after all, show no sign of exploding like tiny Seyfert galaxies, and this weakens the analogy with galactic retarded cores. If the size of such an object is a factor in determining its evolution, it may be that retarded cores of the right mass to act as seeds for the growth of globular clusters are too small to explode. Instead, they remain retarded forever as simple black holes. Or perhaps they burst their bounds very soon after the Big Bang, releasing material which formed into the stars of the globular clusters and settled down into a long life of respectability as quiet collapsed objects. It's still early in the study of cosmic gushers, and it would be ridiculous to claim that the idea can be applied successfully to every kind of object we see in the heavens, although such sweeping claims are generally made when unorthodox theories are first aired.

The Big Flash Theory

One entertaining theory which has run into just this kind of trouble in recent years is the idea that electric forces and discharges may play a significant part in the pattern of the Universe. Dr. C. E. R. Bruce, a member of the Electrical Research Association, has developed this idea and published several papers relating to it, especially in the sixties; in the seventies, the cudgels were taken up on his behalf by E. W. Crew, and evidence—largely photographic—has been gathered in an attempt to persuade doubters that enormous electrical discharges over vast distances and very long times can explain phenomena as diverse as "stellar flares, cosmic jets, quasars, galactic evolution, and much more." As Crew points out, we know that lightning exists on Earth, and, on that basis, the theory is more respectable than the study of black holes, as theorists have yet to be comforted by the unequivocal observational discovery of even one black hole. The superficial appearance of many features observed in astronomical sources, together with this piece of practical experience from the terrestrial atmosphere, is sufficient to get the Bruce theory off the ground. A lightning flash on Earth lasts for a fraction of a second, but multiplying this by a scaling factor equivalent to the size difference between the Earth and Sun gives a flash lasting for an hour or more. Multiply again by a scale factor up to galactic sizes, and flashes can last for millions of years—but how does the electrical charge build up (over an even longer time) before the discharge occurs to produce a jet like those seen in, for example, many quasars? Crew argues that charged particles can be effectively discharged from active galactic nuclei by radiation pressure, producing a charging process through current leakage. Channels through which the cosmic lightning-flashes eventually flow develop into spiral arms, and Seyfert galaxies are an intermediate stage. It's all marvelous speculation, but it becomes quite unbelievable when pushed to extremes. Perhaps there is a grain of truth in the theory—if currents do flow in stellar atmospheres, then discharges must occur in some form or another—even someone with a speculative turn of mind, however, becomes a little doubtful when the theory is invoked to explain changes that have occurred in the Earth's magnetic field over geological time by suggesting that they are linked to "giant discharges in neighboring galaxies." Much as I hate to cast doubt on any theory which gloriously suggests that "strings of galaxies were formed as condensations in the universal discharge channels of the original Big Flash," it is clear that the electrical discharge theory is built from the basic premise that electrical discharges explain *everything,* and this requires the disciple to throw out the baby of a great deal of worthwhile astronomy with the bathwater of a few unexplained phenomena.

This is a valuable lesson to the developer of theories invoking singularities, be they black holes or white. Such extreme ideas are only tenable in circumstances where more conventional ideas have already been tried and failed.

The problem of galaxy formation is a good example with or without a big flash, it is impossible to build galaxies satisfactorily by conventional means in the time available. The big flash idea also suffers because it requires opposite charges—which attract—to separate early, when the Universe is a compact fireball, and to stay separate through a great deal of expansion. So we are forced to consider the possibility of compact retarded cores acting as the seeds of later galaxies. Another problem, the existence of our own Sun, does not require such an extreme solution. There are good theories of how the Sun and other stars can form from collapsing clouds of gas within the overall framework of an established galaxy. Gravity pulls the clouds together, nuclear reactions begin when the center heats sufficiently through gravitational collapse, and from then on the evolution of a star can be explained, in broad outline, quite happily by means of computer simulations, or models. There is no need to invoke the presence of a small black hole at the center of the Sun which might have acted as a seed for the formation of our own star. Such suggestions only cast doubt on the whole idea of the importance of retarded cores in astrophysics, and on the credentials of the suggester. Mind you, at least two different black-hole models of our Sun *have* been proposed, as desperate solutions to the observational puzzle that the Sun emits fewer of the fundamental particles called neutrinos than we would expect if our present theories of stellar structure were perfect. However, since the solar neutrino problem can be resolved in several less drastic ways, the most likely being that the Sun is at present in a slightly disturbed, atypical state resulting from the recent passage of the Solar System through a relatively dense cloud of interstellar material,[2] there is no need here for last resort desperation in the theorizing. (Incidentally, by recent I mean that the Sun passed through an interstellar cloud less than three million years ago—it takes that long for the nuclear pressure cooker in the Sun to adjust to the effects of a disturbance.)

The lesson is clear. An overly hasty attempt to lend weight to a theory by suggesting that it explains everything does the opposite and encourages doubts about those areas where the theory is strong. So you will not find here any dramatic claims that cosmic gushers are the underlying feature directly responsible for everything we see in our Galaxy today; it is impressive enough that such phenomena must be introduced, after discarding all other possibilities, to explain why there is here at all a galaxy in which normal astrophysical processes can begin to operate. And as for explaining reversals of the Earth's magnetic field and geological phenomena such as the Ice Ages and the recent global recession, those can be left to the big flash, proponents of weather lore, and soothsayers.

Galactic Ejections

Where do we draw the line between the end of the direct influence of the cosmic gusher at the center of our Galaxy, which defines the overall structure and sketches in the outline of the Milky Way, and the beginning of what is already the classical view, that is, the realm of everyday astrophysics which has been developed only in the past few decades? The globular clusters, intriguing though they are as a special case, do not provide much help here; nor do the central regions of the Galaxy, which, as in elliptical galaxies, conform with the expected distribution of stars formed in the cloud of gas restrained around any collapsed object present since the earliest time of the Big Bang. We must turn to the spiral structure of the Milky Way, which shows us, as in other spirals, that something has been going on since the initial stage of star formation close to the original retarded core, and which has direct relevance to our place in the Universe since our Solar System is but one insignificant component of the spiral pattern. The Soviet astronomer V. A. Ambartsumian has attempted to produce a unified theory of galaxy and star formation with only limited success. Where his theory is successful, however, it helps to provide insight into the borderland between the influence of the cosmic gusher and the domination of conventional astrophysics. Ambartsumian has compared the distribution of stars in clusters (not globular clusters, but the more open clusters of the spiral arms) and groups with the distribution of galaxies in groups. One of his basic observations is that there are stellar systems in our Galaxy that have positive energy—unlike globular clusters, they are not permanently bound by their own gravity. In particular, such systems often form a so-called trapezium configuration in which there are three equidistant members. Though this is a likely configuration for an expanding system to arrive in, it is an unlikely possibility for any other evolutionary scheme. Some clusters of galaxies also show this trapezium pattern; this is doubly interesting because of the direct implication that they formerly were closer and the implication that they are young systems. The trapezium state is a temporary, early phase, even for expanding systems.

Twenty years ago, Ambartsumian argued from this and other evidence that new galaxies can form by ejection from parent galaxies, with the implication of violent outbursts from galactic nuclei as ejection occurs. We have already seen how much evidence has since accumulated to show that violent outbursts from galactic nuclei occur. Remember also that when Ambartsumian formulated the first versions of his theory quasars had yet to be identified. The most violent activity, which we see as a bright jet ending in a bright condensation, is interpreted by Ambartsumian as the ejection of the nucleus of an embryonic galaxy from its parent. This seems to me a persuasive argument; in terms of the more modern idea of white holes, we would say that the cosmic gusher at the center of a galaxy has fissioned in some way, ejecting a fragment which eventually continues life as a cosmic gusher in its own right. Or, if the nucleus of the parent galaxy originally contained several collapsed objects, one might be shot out through a kind of gravitational slingshot effect. This also gives a neat explanation of such events as the scattering of blue objects in the vicinity of radio galaxy Centaurus A, remarked on by James Terrell. If a white hole split in half like a fissioning amoeba, we might expect two equal sized galaxies to result; at the other extreme, small fragments might be blasted out in a shotgun effect producing a scattering of sources like those in Centaurus

A, which were discovered a good fifteen years after the theory was formulated; in between, there is scope for many interesting intermediate cases. If a large piece of unstable white-hole material is ejected at less than or close to escape velocity, it will move outward, leaving a trail of debris behind—debris which could form the material for development of a spiral-arm structure. Even on a less grandiose scale, high-energy jets of plasma material (atoms stripped into component charged electrons and nuclei) could blast outward into our part of the Galaxy after being formed in explosive phenomena associated with the central cosmic gusher; such streams should, according to the theory, hit the spiral part of the Galaxy about 3,000 or 5,000 parsecs out from the center—and it is just about at 5,000 parsecs that radio astronomy techniques show a great ring of giant clouds of ionized hydrogen. Circumstantial evidence this may be, but it is another small piece of evidence in favor of the cosmic gusher theory. There is one potential snag in the idea. Elliptical galaxies do not seem to rotate very much, and that is firmly in line with the idea that they form in clouds restrained about central retarded cores as the Universe expands. Spiral galaxies definitely do rotate, and something must have set them spinning. In the collapsing gas cloud models, the solution is simple. Even small amounts of rotation present in the large collapsing clouds will create a respectable spin in the smaller galaxy, just as a slowly spinning ice-skater can speed up the spin by drawing the arms in toward the body. With expansion, the effect works the opposite way and galaxies formed by expansion would not be expected to spin much. There are two obvious solutions to this puzzle, and either or both may operate in the real world.

First, any galaxy existing has a good chance of gaining more material from outside because of the influence of its gravitational field, especially if there is a flow of material outward into the universe from active cosmic gushers like those in Seyferts and quasars. It is not true that the only material available for galaxy and star formation is that captured by the retarded core in the earliest period of universal expansion. Accreted matter would, of course, bring its own rotation in to produce a spinning spiral galaxy, as in the collapsing gas cloud model. It is difficult to see where so much material could come from. If enough matter to build a spiral structure is ejected from Seyfert nuclei, the obvious place for it to do the building is in the core of its own galaxy, around the white hole which gave it birth. This, perhaps, makes the second possible resolution of the rotation difficulty more appealing.

Spirals and Companions

Ambartsumian suggests that spiral galaxies form in pairs and that two nuclei forming from one cosmic gusher to become the new pair of spirals split up with an opposite rotation relative to each other. This keeps happily within the laws of physics, since it is permissible for two objects formed in this way to have roughly equal and opposite amounts of angular momentum, as long as the total rotation from the pair averages out as roughly zero to match the rotation of the parent nucleus. In many cases, where angular momentum of close pairs of spiral galaxies has been measured, the total for the pair is indeed very small; and in *all* cases where the two galaxies seem to be physically connected by a bridge of material they rotate in the opposite sense to one another. Such linked pairs are a great puzzle in any other theory of the Universe, as are the intermediate cases in which a spiral galaxy is accompanied by a companion which is small and bright, not showing a spiral structure and lying exactly at the end of a spiral arm.

The classic example is the "whirlpool galaxy," M 51, and its companion. It is appropriate that the study of M 51 first revealed to astronomers the existence of spiral structures in galaxies—hence its name. Photographs of nearby spirals show a clear and beautiful spiral pattern of bright stars, edged by a lane of dark material, sweeping out from the center in two opposite arms. M 51 is a classic example because it is conveniently nearby for study and because it is oriented almost face on to observers on Earth, making study of the spiral pattern very easy. Spectroscopic studies show that the spiral arms themselves are made up mainly of gas and hot young stars (which is true of spirals in general) and that the bridge of material that extends one of the spiral arms of M 51 out to its companion galaxy is made up of just the same kind of material. Radio astronomical studies show the M 51 is also a radio spiral, with two strong spiral arms, detectable at radio frequencies, running along the inner edges of the spiral pattern of bright young stars; this radio evidence, measuring directly the concentration of hydrogen gas by its emission at 21 cm wave length, shows that the arms contain great quantities of hydrogen gas. The bright stars that are obvious in ordinary photographs are merely the by-products of a much greater concentration of material. And, again, the radio evidence clearly reveals this lane of gas extending across the bridge to the companion galaxy. With the evidence from studies of M 51 and other galaxies before them, astronomers can reconstruct the pattern of our own spiral galaxy home, even from the difficult position of making observations from inside that pattern. The companion attached to M 51, however, has long proved an embarrassment to classical theories of the formation and evolution of galaxies, and before we look in more detail at the structure of our Galaxy it is worth quoting the remarks of Bart and Priscilla Bok in the 1974 edition of their book *The Milky Way*:

> Though Messier 51 appears to be one of the prize spiral galaxies, it possesses one structural feature that is in a way very disturbing. This is the companion galaxy, which marks the end of one of the two major spiral arms. Arp has provided good evidence that the companion galaxy is truly associated with Messier 51 and he has furthermore suggested that it was probably ejected from the nucleus of Messier 51 as recently as 10 to 100 million years ago. He considers this observational evidence for a theory of Ambartsumian . . . according to which ejection of mass from the nucleus may be the source of all spiral structure.[3]

Bok and Bok go on to stress that although there is a great deal of variety in the details of the spiral pattern observed in different galaxies, some being tightly wound and others more open, with the only overriding common property being the two trailing spiral arms, "the spiral phenomenon seems to possess a good deal of permanence. If it were a fleeting property of a galaxy we would not expect to find so many of our neighbors showing spiral structure of a very similar type." So our spiral Galaxy is nothing special in the Universe, as we suspected all along, and indeed with the development of ideas about retarded cores and cosmic gushers, it may be that the budding of a companion galaxy from the nucleus of M 51 is nothing special either.

Galactic Components

Successful efforts to trace the spiral structure of our Galaxy, however, only began in the forties when studies of the spiral structure of other galaxies showed that certain types of young stars (O and B stars) are so common in the arms of other spirals that they can be used as tracers in our Galaxy, lighting the path of the spiral arms like street lamps lighting a twisting road. In the fifties, radio astronomy came to the aid of galactic mappers and began to trace the patterns of clouds of hydrogen gas in the Milky Way system, filling in details of the structure invisible to conventional optical telescopes. The result today is that astronomers have a good idea of how our Galaxy would look from the outside— to an observer living on a planet circling a star in one of the spiral arms of M 51—although the picture has not yet been completely resolved because of the great difficulty of getting a view of the whole wood when we are so closely surrounded by the individual trees. Hydrogen clouds, for example, have characteristic velocities due to their participation in the overall rotation and structure of the Galaxy, but they also have individual random velocities, and it is harder to unravel the two from next door than it is when looking across space to another galaxy.

It is clear that the Galaxy consists of three components. The first is the nuclear region, our own central elliptical galaxy, which extends out to about 5,000 parsecs and is surrounded by the second, a thin disc of stars (about 600 parsecs thick at the position of the Solar System) which makes up the spiral pattern. Third, a roughly spherical halo of old stars (and the globular clusters) surrounds the nucleus and disc and seems to be part of the expected pattern of star formation around a retarded core. (Just how far this halo might extend is an open question: studies of M 51 in 1974 showed a surrounding envelope extending across at least 110,000 parsecs, making the size of M 51 on the sky the same as that of our Moon, although the galaxy is vastly further away, almost 10 million light-years compared with the distance to the Moon of about one light-second.) There is also a great curving spur of material which extends out from M 51 around the companion to at least 64,000 parsecs from the nucleus. Studies of other galaxies show similar faint envelopes. The conventional figure for the diameter of our Galaxy is 25,000 parsecs, and that is about right for the extent of the disc of bright stars in which the spiral pattern is obvious. But perhaps we, too, are part of a greater system reaching even farther across space.

Coming closer to home, whatever the overall structure of the Galaxy and the origin of the spiral arms, one thing is clear: our Sun is a second generation star produced by the collapse of a gas cloud within the overall framework of the spiral pattern—a gas cloud, moreover, which contained material that had already been processed through the nuclear furnace operating inside a star at least once. For a picture of our place as the inhabitants of a small planet circling an insignificant star, we need no more than the classical theories of astrophysics developed to explain the origin of the elements in the fifties. On the next step up the scale of the cosmos the central cosmic gusher of our Galaxy becomes important in practical terms as an explanation of why there was material around to condense into stars.

Star Formation

Our picture of how stars form from relatively dense clouds of material in space is fairly complete. Even the protostars of these dense clouds, containing as much as 10,000 million (10^{10}) atoms per cubic centimeter, represent a much more compact, dense collection of material than most of the gas between the stars. In 1975, Professor W. H. McCrea of the University of Sussex explained how such dense clouds could build up from less compact aggregations of matter through repeated encounters with the dark compression lanes of dust and gas which edge the spiral arms. In line with other ideas, McCrea's picture has these dark lanes and the clouds of cool gas revealed by radio astronomy as the real spiral features, with the bright stars of the spiral arms merely by-products of the dark matter. A cloud of gas orbiting the Galaxy under the influence of the gravity of the whole system will pass through the spiral arms and the associated compression lanes twice in each orbit; at each passage, the cloud becomes more compact until it eventually reaches a density sufficient for collapse to continue under its own gravity, and a star (or stars) is born. At the distance of the Solar System from the galactic center, it takes a couple of hundred million years to orbit round the Galaxy once, and, although that is a long time by human standards, it means that the Sun has passed through the spiral compression lanes at least forty times since it formed, and there was ample time for the compacting pre-stellar cloud to encounter the compression lanes several times before that. As today's Solar System has left the compression lane edging the Orion arm of our Galaxy recently (by astronomical standards, that is, within the past 100,000 years) and is about to enter the brightly lit spiral arm proper (where the hot young stars can now be regarded in the light of the new theory as having just been formed in that same compression lane), McCrea's theory is of immediate practical interest. We may even have traveled through the very dense cloud of the Orion nebula. McCrea regards the Sun's present family of comets as a temporary phenomenon, swept up from the gas and dust of the compression lane, soon to be lost again to interstellar space. He even relates the recent passage of the Solar System through the dust and gas of a spiral compression lane to the recent occurrence of an Ice Age on Earth.

Once a protostar does form, gravity will soon pull it together into the hot compact body of a young star. By the time the radius of this ball of gas reaches about 10 to 100 times that of the Sun, it is already beginning to have an internal structure very much like that of an ordinary star, even though the temperature at the surface will still only be about 1,000 or 10,000 degrees;

unlike the Sun, however, such a young star is still powered by gravity. As the large star loses heat from the surface, it collapses into a yet more compact state, and this stage of the collapse, unlike the rush down from an interstellar cloud to a young star, takes a respectable time, several tens of millions of years. Throughout this slow collapse, gravitational energy provides heat which drives the temperature at the center of the star up. When the temperature reaches about ten million degrees, nuclear reactions begin in the interior, fusing hydrogen nuclei together to form helium and providing a source of energy which can halt the collapse. As long as its primary nuclear fuel lasts, the star will now remain in a stable state with a constant brightness and a fixed radius, like our Sun, as a member of the main sequence of stars. But this cannot persist indefinitely, since nuclear fuel, like any other fuel, must eventually run out. For a star like our Sun, eventually is a long, long time—we are safe for thousands of millions of years yet. In time, though, the Sun will end its life as a white dwarf (it is too small to end as a neutron star or black hole and has no companion to exchange mass with, fortunately for us). How will it reach this fate?

Star Death

The first steps up the fusion ladder of nuclear processes are simple. Two hydrogen nuclei combine to form a nucleus of deuterium (heavy hydrogen) with the emission of a positron; deuterium and hydrogen in turn combine to form helium-3, which contains two protons and one neutron in each nucleus, and two helium-3 nuclei combine to make one nucleus of helium-4 (two protons; two neutrons) with emission of two hydrogen nuclei (protons) to go back into the pot. This process keeps the Sun hot because the mass of the end product (a helium-4 nucleus) is less than the mass of the ingredients (two hydrogen nuclei). The balance goes as heat, following $E = mc^2$. The energy produced in the Sun today is equivalent to the destruction of 4.6 million tons of mass every second, a mere fleabite compared with the mass of the Sun, which is 2,000-billion billion tons. Other elements are also built up in the stellar interior, although the net fusing of hydrogen into helium dominates at this stage. Helium builds up in the core; the supply of hydrogen fuel diminishes and eventually becomes insufficient to provide enough energy to hold up the star. Then, a curious change occurs.

As energy production decreases, the core contracts and heats up through the release of gravitational energy. With a hotter center, there is a greater outward pressure, and the outer layers of the star actually expand so that the star becomes a red giant with a radius hundreds of times that of the Sun. Meanwhile, in the hotter core, a new series of fusion reactions begins when the temperature reaches about 100 million degrees; with helium as the fuel, these reactions build up many elements such as carbon, oxygen, neon, and magnesium. From now on, the details of the evolution of a star are not thoroughly understood, but it seems that helium burning can certainly be followed by one further stage of nuclear burning, with carbon nuclei as the fuel. It is at this stage, too, that a giant star can become very involved with any companion it may have, through mass transfer. And this transfer of mass may explain why in some stars the nuclear burning in the core suddenly produces a supernova explosion.

The end of our Sun probably won't be the bang of a supernova but the whimper of quiet collapse, when all nuclear burning possibilities have been used, with the Sun then settling into the white dwarf state. There is the intermediate possibility of a nova, an explosion on a smaller scale than a supernova. This is the fate of many stars. Indeed, the fact that it has already been the fate of whole generations of stars may be fortunate since we are the by-products of those stellar explosions. Apart from hydrogen and a little helium produced in the Big Bang, every atom of every element has been built up by nuclear fusion reactions in the stellar pressure cookers. The elements only arrive in interstellar space and mingle in the clouds of forming protostars through nova and supernova explosions, eventually providing a significant fraction of the material in second-generation protostars, with some of the heavy elements ending up in planets. There could be no planets without heavy elements, so the first generation of stars in any galaxy must have been entirely planetless. After many stellar explosions, there is enough heavy material around to allow formation of planetary systems as new stars form, and, with plenty of elements to build complex systems from, the prospect for life to evolve on some of those planets. We are, literally, star children, and the carbon, oxygen, and other elements vital to life were made inside stars. Only the hydrogen in our water is leftover from the spectacular event of the Big Bang, and it is quite possible that many of those hydrogen nuclei have been through the nuclear fusion process inside stars, later being ejected as protons from more complicated atomic nuclei. This raises the intriguing possibility that elliptical galaxies may be devoid of life.

It is a simple matter to account for the formation of stars in the dense cloud of material restrained around the retarded core of a potential cosmic gusher as the Universe expands, but difficult to explain how second-generation stars can form in galaxies as they exist today. McCrea's theory, which depends very much on the spiral structure of our Galaxy, is the best yet available, and the wealth of observational information about collapsing gas clouds and young star systems in our Galaxy points to spiral arms as the birthplaces of stars, regardless of the exact details of any specific theory. Bok and Bok, referring to the spiral arms of our own and neighboring galaxies, had this to say:

> Many dark nebulae and globules composed of interstellar gas and dust are seen almost in the act of collapsing into protostars or their close relatives. Objects that are either protostars or very young stars have also been observed. Infrared objects provide a natural link between small dark clouds and relatively normal stars. Quite a few of them may be cool, dense dust clouds with a star or a cluster of stars near the center.[4]

None of this applies to elliptical galaxies. Only in spirals like our own do we see regions of activity where material from stellar explosions can mix, form new clouds, and condense into second-generation stars with planets and associated life. And all the evidence is that the spiral structure of our own and other galaxies is the most direct product of the activity of the central cosmic gusher. Without such a gusher, there would still be the nucleus and halo of our Galaxy, devoid of planets and life. With the gusher, we have spiral structure, a veritable melting pot for redistribution of the elements, second and later generations of stars, and planets on which life can evolve. We are more than just star children; we owe our very existence to the presence of a cosmic gusher at the center of our Galaxy.

5
WHY SHOULD A WHITE HOLE GUSH?

It is a remarkable coincidence, if indeed it is a coincidence, that the most dense and massive objects visible in our Universe are without exception expanding rapidly and pouring out great quantities of energy. Standard ideas, whether those of Newtonian or Einsteinian physics, suggest rather that these concentrations of matter should be collapsing under the influence of their own gravitational fields; the implication, as Fred Hoyle pointed out during the sixties, is that conventional theories must break down when they are applied to such objects as galactic nuclei and quasars, which, as we now see, may be the same thing viewed at different times. For many years, Hoyle's advocacy of this extreme course of action was far from welcomed by other astronomers, let alone those physicists who work in the more comfortable familiarity of laboratory experiments. With the breakthrough of less conventional ideas having become acceptable in the wake of the remarkable observations of strange sources by satellites monitoring X-rays and gamma rays, and with speculation about black holes now respectable, the idea that a new physics—or a new development of the old physics—may be needed to explain the most energetic events in the Universe is no longer frowned upon. To get attention for such ideas, it helps if one is a Fred Hoyle of science, but lesser mortals can get a hearing for unconventional views, even if those views are not always taken seriously. Some of the ideas that have been touted seem ridiculous, but we must be prepared to consider them. We do not know why a white hole should gush. We can make great progress in explaining energetic phenomena in terms of cosmic gushers, or white holes, but only by assuming that something has started the gusher off. It is much like accepting that the Universe exists and that it originated in a Big Bang, without knowing why or how the Big Bang was set off. Whether we are examining the origin of the Universe or the cause of the explosions in Seyfert galaxies, this is unsatisfactory, but progress is being made. As we shall see in Part III, there are plausible theories about the nature of the Big Bang and the origin of the Universe, theories which tell much about the likely future of the Universe. On the smaller scale of white-hole explosions in galaxies and quasars, there are some clear signposts for theorists.

Two-Component Theories

One idea—a good signpost for a route *not* to take—is the theory that the violent outbursts in many astronomical objects are the result of previous collapses which have bounced at a critical high density. One form of this theory was developed by Hoyle and Narlikar a decade ago, using the mathematical system they originally developed in the context of a Steady State theory. Their idea was to split the mathematical description of gravity into two components. One component arises from the interaction of the whole universe of matter with local regions of space-time, and the other depends on local conditions only becoming important at very great densities. Such a theory can easily be juggled to produce a situation in which ordinary gravity first dominates a collapsing system, but, at a critical density, the second component of the gravity field switches in to produce a violent repulsion which blasts material back in a great explosion. As the second component has never been measured, the numbers can be chosen to fit any given observation of astrophysical explosions.

Though this line of reasoning scarcely seems worth following up, it seems to have fascinated some mathematicians. As recently as December 1975 another pair of relativists, Joe and Nathan Rosen, published a similar theory claiming to do away with black holes. Any theory which purports to remove the possibility of black-hole singularities at a stroke and also offers an explanation of quasars and Seyferts is worthy of noting, even if it seems dubious. The Rosen-Rosen theory depends upon two components in the mathematical formulation of the field equations, with one component describing everyday gravitational effects and the other bringing in inertial forces.

When the two-component theory is applied to the problem of the stability of a cold neutron star—which, you may remember, is the key to black-hole formation in other theories—the exact results depend on how much of the second component you mix into the model. Whereas relativity predicts that a cold star of more than three solar masses must collapse first into a black hole and then into a singularity, the Rosen-Rosen theory allows stability for masses in a range six to twelve times that of the Sun. If one accepts the model, it explains the existence of a compact neutron star, rather than a black hole, in the famous source Cygnus X-1. But it does not explain the very rapid flickering of that source, the best real evidence for the presence of a black hole. Aside from that, Rosen-Rosen neutron stars will collapse if they become more massive. The question is, just what form does such a collapse take? The Rosens say that their theory "does not admit black holes," but even Newtonian theory admits black holes, and holds that any dense object will be invisible if its surface gravity is so great that light cannot escape. What the Rosen-Rosen equations indicate is that, in their model, collapsing stars more massive than twelve solar masses do not disappear into a singularity but turn inside out, as it were, collapsing right through themselves and becoming expanding objects. It's an interesting speculation, especially considering the possibility of such collapsing-expanding objects being temporary but nonsingular black holes.

During the critical moments when the star turns inside out it will be inside a quite ordinary Newtonian event horizon, as far as particles are concerned, so that the trick, like most magic tricks, will take place out of sight of the audience. First a collapsar, then an expandar.

What will this sort of gusher look like? While everything is jammed into a tiny volume, conditions must be very much like the fireball in which the Universe began. As re-expansion begins, nothing can escape until the critical density is reached. Matter and radiation must be intermingled, as in the early moments of the life of the Universe. As soon as the density decreases sufficiently for the escape velocity to drop below that of light, radiation and energetic particles blast away at or just under the speed of light, with most of the mass following at less dramatic speeds. A good massive object, such as one of 100,000 million solar masses, as the initial collapsar might make the end product look very much like a Seyfert galaxy or a quasar. How all that mass would be involved in a collapse is essentially the same problem as that of the origin of galaxies in the expanding Universe. There is no plausible way of accounting for the collapse of objects that massive from a roughly uniform cloud of expanding material, and once a retarded core or something similar is added to hold things together, the inside-out theory of cosmic explosions is no longer needed. The mathematicians get an "A" for their ingenuity of equation juggling but a raspberry for forgetting the physical realities of the real Universe.

The White Hole and Universal Gushers

The analogy between the white-hole gusher and the universal gusher can, however, productively be pushed a long way as it is possible to describe what an exploding gusher or a white hole should look like under different circumstances. Narlikar has remained active in the study of this kind of object, in recent years producing a series of fascinating papers with colleagues at the Tata Institute in Bombay. In one particularly significant paper, published in 1975. Narlikar and Professor K. M. V. Apparáo took a mathematical look at the possible relationships between different sizes of white holes and the whole range of puzzling phenomena now plaguing high-energy astrophysicists. As the basis of their work they accept that an exploding white hole might exist, just as in cosmology we accept that the expanding Universe exists, and they look at the kind of electromagnetic spectrum that should be produced by a white hole, taking into account the inevitable blue shift of the radiation. The early stages follow the same equations as those of the Einstein–de Sitter cosmology which we have already used in calculating the behavior of a retarded core on the scale of a galaxy. Unlike some mathematicians, Narlikar and Apparao are adept at explaining the implications of their equations in terms of the physics of the processes involved.

White-hole explosions are both violent and short-lived, and Narlikar and Apparao state that it is natural to see if they can explain some of the explosive and transient phenomena observed in astronomy. Although the effects of white-hole behavior on the electromagnetic radiation produced can be calculated, exactly what kind of radiation is being produced inside the white hole cannot. There is doubt about how the theoretical spectrum of electromagnetic radiation can be made to fit the observed spectrum of radiation from explosive and transient astronomical sources, but, given the assumptions involved, it wouldn't be appropriate to push the theory too far in its present form. One key feature of the observed explosive transient events is that they initially have hard spectra, dominated by high-energy radiation, which then soften as more low-energy radiation emerges. This is also what would happen to radiation emerging from a white hole. The more blue-shifted radiation would emerge first into the visible universe. The largest scale of explosion Narlikar and Apparao considered was a Seyfert galaxy, where it seems that there is enough energy available in roughly the right kind of state to power the explosions. This ties in with the ideas about retarded cores already mentioned, but the exciting new results emergent from the paper by Narlikar and Apparao concern transient phenomena within our Galaxy. It seems that small white holes may be popping off from time to time throughout the Milky Way.

Transient X-ray sources show a sudden rise to peak energy, a subsequent softening of the spectrum, and an overall "power law" type of spectrum, in line with the white-hole theory. Between one X-ray source and another there are significant spectral differences, but they all fall within the range of modified spectra to be expected if the white-hole effect is distorting the electromagnetic radiation which starts out inside the white hole as one of the three standard forms of radiation known in astrophysical processes: black-body radiation (like the microwave background); free-free radiation (produced by interactions between charged particles); or synchrotron radiation (produced when charged particles interact with strong magnetic fields). Gamma radiation in bursts of the kind unexpectedly detected by satellite experiments in the early seventies can be explained as a white-hole effect, and even the production of high-energy particles, which might be the background of cosmic rays, is likely to occur as matter blasts out from a white hole.

What would this leave behind? The energy required for a transient X-ray source suggests that the mass left-over would be a few solar masses; if this mass were in the form of hydrogen with a sprinkling of other elements, it could become a star lost amidst the billions of other stars of the Milky Way. For gamma-ray bursts, the end product might be a white dwarf of one solar mass. There is the seductive possibility that a majority of stars could have emerged in this way but at the present state of the theory, there is danger of falling into the all-too-common trap of thinking a new idea can explain everything. It is worthy of note, however, that these mathematically based ideas tie in with the physically based ideas of astronomers such as Ambartsumian who have looked closely at the evidence of expansion and fragmentation among astronomical systems. It is even more noteworthy that the immediate success of the Narlikar-Apparao calculations, when they are applied in the context of the real Universe and especially our Galaxy, has come from a very simple version of white-hole mathematics. Still, the theory has yet to be developed as black-hole theory has been, to take into account the effect of electrical charge and the influence of non-spherical distributions of matter.

Narlikar and Apparao seem to keep open minds on whether the origin of material from a white hole implies that it has emerged from a singularity, and Narlikar, in particular, has never failed to point out the similarity between the appearance of matter from white holes and the creation of matter, as is required by modified forms of the Steady State theory. It may well be that conventional physics is inadequate to describe the earliest stages of white-hole expansion, whether on the scale of a gamma-ray burst or on the scale of the whole Universe; in my view, it is unlikely that even a drastically modified Steady State theory is a plausible explanation of the real Universe. But all such questions are of no relevance to the fact that the calculations of white-hole explosion effects produce results much like the explosive transient phenomena observed in the real Universe in the region where conventional relativity theory does seem to apply. To draw an analogy, you do not have to believe in God in order to appreciate the beauty of many works created in God's name, nor do you have to be an atheist to accept the reality of the evolution of the species.

Black-Hole Explosions

A serious problem for the Narlikar-Apparao work, as for other white-hole studies, is D. M. Eardley's suggestion that lagging cores become unstable as they accrete matter and may turn into black holes before they get around to exploding. This may be a sure indication that a better physics is needed, since the whole question of when and why a retarded core explodes outward is intimately related to the boundary conditions of the event in which the expanding Universe was created. Since we don't know anything about the creation event, we don't know what special boundary conditions may rule the initial lesser creation events of white-hole explosions. Eardley's is one of the clearest signposts for the direction of future research; if mathematicians can tell us more about the stability of white holes in general, then we will be much better able to relate the possible existence of white holes to events in the real Universe. Narlikar and Apparao have summed up the situation regarding white-hole explosions in the light of our understanding in the mid-seventies:

> It seems to us that we are in a somewhat similar situation with regard to the existence of white holes as existed for black holes about a decade ago. Then there were objections to supermassive objects forming on the grounds of angular momentum and fragmentation difficulties. In spite of these objections, gravitational collapse of supermassive objects was studied for various reasons, including the important one that the presence of QSOs indicates the existence of compact massive systems. We feel that the evidence of exploding objects in the Universe (including perhaps the Universe itself if it started with a Big Bang) indicates the necessity of studying white holes in the astrophysical context in spite of any possible stability problem seen at present.[1]

If the possibility that potential white holes might turn into black holes remains a question in the minds of some relativists, this is more than compensated for by the amazing discovery in the mid-seventies that black holes can explode. Indeed, any black hole must eventually explode, according to our present understanding of the equations—the question is, when? This dramatic discovery emerged from a study of the nature of black holes by the young mathematician Stephen Hawking—surely the most able relativist of his generation, with a fine grasp of physical reality—and his colleagues. They attempted to develop an understanding of black holes in terms of four basic laws, equivalent to or transcending the four laws of thermodynamics. The direction of this work is important to current and future research and may lead to an eventual combination of the ideas of relativity, statistical mechanics, and quantum mechanics that could be the development of a new physics to explain high-energy events involving large masses and high densities. A single insight from Hawking, that black holes explode (or, as he has put it, "black holes aren't black"), is sufficient to emphasize the way our picture of fundamental universal processes has changed within the recent past.

At its simplest, the discovery that black holes can interact with the outside Universe and radiate away energy until they are no longer massive enough to remain stable black holes depends on the basic interchangeability of mass and energy. Any sufficiently strong energy field can, in principle, lead to the spontaneous creation of particles as the energy present in a small volume is converted to matter occupying the same volume. This process always involves the production of pairs of particles, a particle, such as an electron, and its equivalent antiparticle, such as a positron. In this way, the various laws of conservation of electric charge, momentum, and so on are maintained, even though matter and energy interchange. The paired particles can collide quickly with one another and be mutually annihilated, their mass being converted back into energy as electromagnetic radiation. One of the curious features of quantum theory is that pairs of particles can be produced in this way even when the background energy density is low, provided that they annihilate one another within a very short time. This depends on the uncertainty principle named after Heisenberg, which, in everyday terms, states that we cannot be certain that there is insufficient energy available for a particle pair to exist for a tiny fraction of a second; therefore, they *can* exist for that brief interval, and the vacuum of space could be full of particle pairs flicking in and out of existence. Such a situation—known as vacuum fluctuations—has little practical relevance, but it may be relevant to the question of the existence of the whole Universe, as we shall see in Chapter 8. For the time being, however, it is sufficient that, if the energy density in a small region of space is great enough, then pairs of particles can be created. Since even photons (light particles) and neutrinos count as particles as far as the quantum mechanical equations are concerned, the energy involved need not be ridiculously high, even allowing for the daunting factor of c^2 in Einstein's well-known equation.

Particle Creation and the Event Horizon

Just outside a black hole, there is a very strong gravitational field which contains a lot of energy. What could be more natural, in the light of quantum theory, than that particles should be produced in pairs near the black-hole horizon? In retrospect, it is obvious—but it took a Hawking to work through the mathematics for the first time and point out the obvious. However, it is less than obvious what happens to a pair of particles created just outside the black hole. An odd feature of black holes is that sometimes, when a particle is dropped into one, the particle can take up an orbit around the central singularity which corresponds to negative binding energy. A satellite put into a negative-energy orbit around the Earth would fly off into space; but as nothing can escape from a black hole, a particle which drops into such a strange situation is stuck with it—and so is the black hole. What this means in practical terms is that it is possible for the *addition* of a particle to a black hole to result in a *loss* of energy. It is now easy to see what can happen to a pair of particles created just outside the black hole's horizon. One falls in, with energy lost; the other picks up the energy, which is conserved overall, and uses it to scoot away into space. The net result is that the black hole bubbles quietly away, radiating energy in the form of energetic particles such as photons and neutrinos. And when it loses enough energy (that is, mass) so that its gravity is no longer sufficient to maintain it as a black hole, the event horizon disappears and highly compressed hot material comes blasting outward—just like a white hole.

This very simple outline does not do justice to theories developed by Hawking and others; this is one of those cases where mere words are insufficient and the full beauty of the theory can only be seen in mathematical terms. The results, however, are very clear and can be understood in simple physical terms. First, although it might so far seem that all problems about retarded cores and white-hole explosions have been solved and that everything we have been dealing with might be explained as a black-hole explosion, that is far from the case. The main snag is that the lifetime of a black hole before it explodes depends on how much mass-energy it must lose before the explosion occurs, and for massive black holes this lifetime would be much longer than the currently accepted figure for the lifetime of the whole Universe. If black holes were to explode as the retarded cores we need for galaxy formation, they would still be retarded today, and we would not see any galaxies, nor, to be accurate, would we be here to do any observing. Small black holes might be ready to explode by now, but how would they have formed in the first place? A lot of compression is needed to produce a low-mass black hole, and, as it happens, Hawking had already considered this in his earlier work, notably with B. J. Carr. The one place in the Universe where conditions would have been right for creating mini black holes was the Big Bang.

Black-Hole Masses— Large and Small

I have made much of the fact that we can only apply our best theories, such as relativity, from some definite time after the creation singularity—assuming there was a creation singularity—and this seems a good place to put some numbers on the length of that unknowable initial instant. By bringing in the uncertainty principle and thinking in terms of the wave length of the Universe, we have developed the generally accepted rule of thumb that the earliest time at which we can apply relativity, at least, in its classical formulation, is 10^{-43} of a second after the singularity. That is, classical relativity is only a good description of the Universe since the first ten-millionth of a billion-billion-billion-billionth of a second after the start of the Big Bang! The trouble is that all the interesting boundary conditions relate to that crucial initial instant. At that earliest moment for which our best theories today can be applied, any black holes formed would have masses of only one hundred-thousandth of a gram and radii of only 10^{-33} cm—the smallest (that is, least massive) black holes that could ever have existed in the Universe as we know it. Looking ahead to more reasonable times, a black hole formed at the time of helium formation, when the temperature of the Universe was about 1,000 million degrees, compared with its present-day 2.7 degrees, would have a much more respectable mass equivalent of 10 million suns. There are interesting puzzles for the mathematicians studying what might happen to this kind of object. For example, would they grow by accreting mass faster than they lose energy by pair production? In the light of Hawking's work, an intriguing category of these primordial black holes is the intermediate, between supermassive black holes, which grow by accretion so fast that they don't ever explode, and mini black holes, which are so small that they exploded long ago.

The radius of a black hole is proportional to its mass, and its temperature, that is, the rate at which it radiates energy, as determined by Hawking, is inversely proportional to its mass, so that bigger black holes by radiating less energy have a lower effective temperature. A black hole the size of a proton would contain about 10^{15} (1,000 billion) grams. Holes of that size, perhaps up to 1,000 times bigger, ought to have lifetimes roughly comparable to the age of the Universe. Near the end of its life as a black hole, such an object would radiate energy at a very high rate, so that in the last tenth of a second, as it exploded, about 10^{30} ergs of energy would be liberated. That is small beer by astronomical standards—the Sun radiates 3,000 times as much energy every second—but it is still equivalent to the simultaneous explosion of about a million one-megaton nuclear bombs. For holes 1,000 times bigger, a comparably greater amount of energy could be liberated in the final stages, and, if there are large numbers of black holes in our Galaxy, explosions in this range would certainly be detectable. Once again, speculators have been quick to link this idea with the mysterious, recently discovered gamma-ray bursts. Mathematically, there is little to choose between a black hole that has evaporated to the point where it explodes and a retarded mini core that suddenly bursts forth as a white hole. The calculations of Narlikar and Apparao need but little modification to be applied to the case of exploding black holes.

In its standard form, this theory, as developed by Hawking, is of only minor interest in the framework of the violent activity observed on much greater scales in exploding galaxies, quasars, and so on. Conceptually, however, the theory is probably one of the most significant advances since the realization that the Universe expands, and the new lines of research it has opened up could prove the most fruitful of all in taking our understanding of the Universe a stage farther. Exploding black holes cannot, however, explain the presence of the most violent objects known in the Universe, unless our detailed understanding of the time-scale of the Universe or of black-hole explosions is wrong. In any case, it does seem that the largest black holes would gain energy from accretion faster than they would radiate it, like a tub being filled from a powerful hose more quickly than the water can drain away through a small leak. We certainly should not rule out the possibility that our present understanding of these phenomena is inaccurate. Some recent speculations provide examples of how physical speculation with insufficient recourse to rigorous mathematics can be as seductive and as potentially misleading as beautiful mathematical models having little or no grounding in physical reality.

Depending on the elementary particle physics and quantum mechanical element in a study of exploding black holes, and leaving aside the time-scale problem and the question of rapid accretion of very large holes, an idea of what the material blasting out from such an explosion should be like can be built up. The most intriguing possibility is that instead of being gamma-ray bursts at about 10^{30} ergs in 0.1 s, the explosions might be bursts of particles of many different kinds, releasing 10^{35} ergs (100,000 times more energy) in 10^{-23} s (100 billion-billionths of 0.1 s). The description of an event like this for times after that critical 10^{-23} s is very similar to the cosmological description of the expansion of the Universe of particles and radiation after the initial tiny fraction of a second. Now, if you follow the Hoyle type of argument to preserve a form of Steady State theory by imagining a Universe which is Steady State on the really big scale but looks like a Big Bang on the scale of all the visible galaxies and quasars, there is room for a neat but implausible trick. In a truly infinite Steady State universe, there is infinite time and infinite space available for a very big black hole to grow, one containing as much mass as the observable Universe in which we live. Speculating wildly and brushing aside quibbles about accretion, this grand-scale black hole could explode outward again, after a long enough wait, producing something very much like the expanding region of space we see around us. It's easy to shoot down such naive speculation—the accretion problem, the question of how much mass would actually be left when the giant hole exploded (since it would have been radiating energy for an awesomely long time), and so on. Wilder ideas have been aired and have gained devotees who publish learned papers about them in respectable journals. Part of the attraction of cosmology is the opportunity for grand speculation. As you can see, some of this speculation is too far out to reach the pages of even a science-fiction magazine. The importance of exploding black holes in the development of ideas about cosmic gushers is chiefly that their possible existence emphasizes that the whole concept of white-hole explosions is not entirely ridiculous. The definitive answer to the question of why a white hole should gush (or where the gusher gets its material) is not yet available, and it would probably justify a Nobel Prize. Meanwhile, some speculations less far out than those outlined above could fit into a science-fiction story and provide a plausible way of relating the white-hole creation event to some of the more rigorous calculations of mathematicians such as Narlikar and Apparao.

Tree Trunks and Trousers

I first encountered the concept of space-time trousers in 1969 at the Institute of Theoretical Astronomy in Cambridge during a conference on relativity and related topics. The highlight, for me, of that meeting was a discussion of white holes. It was sparked by the problem of where the material being ejected from quasars and nuclei of objects such as N-galaxies and Seyferts comes from: could it be pouring into our Universe through holes in space? At that meeting W. Büdich, from Göttingen, offered a neat mathematical model that included treatment of such an effect, showing that the sudden appearance of matter in our visible Universe can be explained within the framework of relativity. In view of recent developments in the study of both black and white holes, his ideas seem even more apposite today.

Since we cannot build four-dimensional models showing variations of the theoretical Universe in both space and time, and since our drawings are restricted to two-dimensional paper and blackboards, astronomers use a simplified space-time diagram in which one direction (up the page or board) represents the flow of time and the other (across the page or board) represents movement through space. Extending this to represent space by a series of planes at right angles to the paper, and with a little skill in perspective drawing, it is possible to represent three space and one time dimensions as two space and one time dimensions drawn in just two dimensions. The easy way to picture the Universe in this way is like the trunk of a tree. We are somewhere in the middle, unable to see the edges of the tree's surface. The flow of time is equivalent to moving upward through the trunk. Imagine what the space-time equivalent of a fork in the tree would be. Suppose we sat in galaxy A next door to another galaxy, B, moving up through the trunk until upon reaching the fork each galaxy moved into a separate arm of the fork. Now, confined as we would be, within limits of one branch instead of the whole trunk, we would believe that galaxy B had disappeared—fallen into a black hole. Repeated branches of the space-time tree would be equivalent to the way pessimistic cosmologists imagine the fate of the real Universe—for it to be gobbled up in a series of black holes. At the first fork and the tree trunk, the space-time picture gives the appearance of a fat letter Y, or of a catapult. (See figure 2.) Now, in order to account for the sudden appearance of matter in our Universe we can run the whole thing in reverse—or, which is just as good, turn the picture upside-down. The two branches now form the fat legs of a pair of trousers, merging into an even fatter waist. And the journey of galaxy A up one leg of the trousers will bring it to a spectacular moment when all the material of the other leg pops into view.

The analogy with Seyferts or quasars is not yet exact —we do not see whole galaxies emerging intact from another branch of space-time. However, if we make the other leg of the trousers very thin, or at least restrict its width where it joins the waist, we can imagine matter being squirted through in energetic fashion. A better analogy might be to treat the mainstream of space-time, our visible Universe, as a broad, onward-flowing river, joined by many rushing streams that plummet downward from surrounding mountains. Either way, new material has, to all intents and purposes, been created in our Universe.

Although these analogies are only a poor representation of the reality of the mathematics, once again the physical intuition of the simple pictures and the hard reality of the mathematical equations go hand in hand. The analogy can be stretched further by relating the

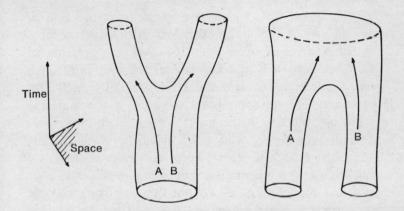

Figure 2

Left: The Y space-time. Galaxies move into separate branches of space as time goes by.

Right: Space-time trousers. By reversing the direction of time, new material pops out into the visible universe as time goes by.

Big Bang creation to the upwelling of the source of our space-time river in some great spring—a real cosmic gusher. The most important thing is that, within the framework of relativity theory, it is possible to envisage a space-time with branches joining the mainstream and material flowing in and out of our knowledge. Indeed, space-time as we know it may in itself be only a tributary; we may already have branched off from the mainstream and be stuck in a universal dead end.

With all of this, we have not discussed the role of singularities, white or black holes, in this picture of a branching river of space-time. However, the evidence of the violent events is that new matter squeezes in through very small holes, even if the holes are not exactly singularities. This multiple-branch model of the Universe is flexible; the size of the mouth of each tributary is essentially immaterial. A more complex, but easily understandable, model of the Universe also rests on a secure foundation of mathematics. For some exotic trees, the root and branch systems do not fan out from a single main trunk but are joined and rejoined to one another —multiply connected. There are aspects of both the branching Y space-time and the multiply joined version of space-time trousers in the same system. Matter can both disappear into branches and emerge from tributaries, and the same material can disappear into a hole in one part of space-time only to re-emerge from a gusher in another part of space-time. In a multiply connected universe, the answer to the question, why does a white hole gush? is because something fell into a black hole somewhere else at some other time.

Hyperspace

The idea of multiply connected universes and tunnels through space-time has been around in a respectable mathematical form since 1962 when John Wheeler's *Geometrodynamics* was published. In science fiction, however, the idea is even older. In 1942, the first part of what was to become the classic "Foundation" trilogy was published in *Astounding Science Fiction*. A passage in the book version, published nine years later, suggests that Isaac Asimov[2] was one of the first to recognize the potentialities of hyperspace.

> He had steeled himself just a little for the Jump through hyper-space, a phenomenon one did not experience in simple interplanetary trips. The Jump remained, and would probably remain forever, the only practical method of traveling between the stars. Travel through ordinary space could proceed at no rate more rapid than that of light (a bit of scientific knowledge that belonged among the few items known since the forgotten dawn of human history), and that would have meant years of travel between even the nearest of inhabited systems. Through hyper-space, that unimaginable region that was neither space nor time, matter nor energy, something nor nothing, one could traverse the length of the Galaxy in the intervals between two neighboring instants of time.

Maybe Asimov wasn't actually the first writer to use the idea, but his stories seem to be the oldest which both mention hyperspace and are still in print three decades later, and that is worthy of recognition in itself.

When mathematicians began to catch up with Asimov in the sixties, they coined the word superspace for what amounts to the same thing as hyperspace. I prefer hyperspace. The sixties version of hyperspace is less unimaginable than the original. No longer neither matter nor energy, the fabric through which our observable Universe tunnels, perhaps in a multiply connected way, is described by Wheeler and others as built up from gravitational particles (geons, by analogy with light particles or photons) which contain both mass and energy, even though they are built of curved empty space.

Even in the modern mathematical form, hyperspace is timeless, a region in which before and after have no meaning. If a traveler could be sent into hyperspace and back out into another part of our Universe, no time would have elapsed for him even though he might seem to us to have traveled many light-years. It might be difficult to decide *when* and *where* and *how* to get out of hyperspace, once in it. A shortcut through the honeycombs of hyperspace, a wormhole which would take the traveler out of a local region of space-time and cut across a corner to another region of the same tunnel in which we live, or even into a different tunnel, would be ideal. This is a familiar science-fiction idea, one which now looks to be a practicable possibility, if not for us today then for someone else someday. It is tempting to invent a rule of thumb about the relation of science-fiction ideas to relativists' ideas which are pushing our understanding of the Universe to the limit. The most extravagant notions of the science-fiction writers regarding space-time are probably practicable, merely needing engineering

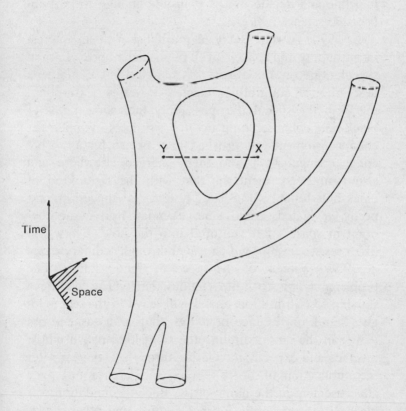

Figure 3

A multiply connected space-time. To travel from X to Y requires traveling backward in time for part of the journey or tunneling through hyperspace (dotted line).

solutions to become reality. The most extravagant ideas of the relativists, on the other hand, are too ridiculous to be taken seriously by science-fiction writers or readers.

An exaggeration? Perhaps. But try the following factual tale and decide if it is plausible enough to be published as science fiction.

In 1974, Adrian Berry, a journalist with an interest in astronomy and space travel, published a book of grand speculations on the future of mankind.[3] It contains a description of multiply connected universes. Extrapolating from the speculative possibility that some kinds of black-hole collapse could involve a process in which the collapsing object was crushed (but not so far as to become a singularity) and then emerged elsewhere and elsewhen, Berry mentions that with the right kind of black-hole-tunnel-white-hole system "a spaceship, expertly navigated, could emerge undamaged at another point in space" if it ventured into the hole. Berry also discusses space ships which travel through ordinary space at 99.999 percent of the speed of light, saying, "The problem of *how* to build engines that will accelerate a starship to 670 million mph I will leave to the technologists," and, on the face of things, that is an easier problem than the one of finding the right kind of wormhole in space and expertly navigating through it. A year after the publication of Berry's book, in 1975, a full page advertisement in the name of the Bacon Foundation was placed in the scientific journal *Nature,* and other magazines, offering a reward of £300 to the person or persons who provided a solution to the following problem:

According to current theory, rotating black holes are actually gateways to other regions of space-time. How, therefore, could a space vehicle pass through a rotating black hole into another region of space-time without being crushed by the gravitational field of a singularity?

The advertisement also offered computer time to serious contenders for the prize, and, as far as I know, the prize is still unclaimed and the offer is still open. Lest you should be tempted by it, remember that even with free computer time, the prize is a bit miserly as a reward for the invention of a true space-drive to the stars! Now, I am quite sure any science-fiction editor I know would have dismissed the story of such an offer as ridiculous and implausible if it had been offered to him in 1974.

The Naked Singularity

There is something in this tale of rotating black holes as possible gateways to the stars. A collapsing object shaped like an American football and rotating about its long axis would be crushed into a long, thin, threadlike singularity *without* being surrounded by an event horizon. The singularity would be visible and free to interact with the outside Universe—a naked singularity. Information about the singularity could leak out along the thread which would make a hole in any imaginable event horizon surrounding it. If naked singularities exist, they provide loopholes in the conventional understanding of our Universe as an orderly place in which effects always follow causes. The interaction of a naked singularity with the outside world could produce regions in which, by comparison with events here on Earth, time runs backward and effects occur before the actions which cause them. Causality, as we know it, here breaks down. Some relativists apply a cosmic censorship by arguing that, because naked singularities would imply the breakdown of causality, they must be impossible. Others are sanguine about the prospect, not least since, if we found a naked singularity, its properties could tell us much about the origin of the Universe, itself a naked singularity as far as we are concerned. As Roger Penrose [4] has put it, "The initial mystery of creation then would no longer be able to hide in the obscurity afforded by its supposed uniqueness," a sentiment that carries over into the consideration of white holes in general. A few doomsayers, led by John Taylor of King's College, London, are filled with terrible forebodings by the prospect of finding a naked singularity. Taylor says:

> It is that which could destroy our orderly universe. It could be that only by construction of such a monstrosity would we ever learn what really does happen to matter at the final stage of collapse to a nonexistent point. If so, it would be a hard price to pay—the end of our own world—for discovering what such a finale really is.[5]

A tame naked singularity, or rotating black hole, which only perturbs causality locally, could be a very interesting phenomenon. Taylor discussed that prospect in the light of the Bacon Foundation offer in a radio broadcast during Christmas week 1975 and, in keeping with the festive spirit of the time, the interpretation he offered was much less gloomy than some of his published prognostications. With a collapsed, rotating black hole there is, it seems, a ring of singularity which can be avoided by the expert navigation suggested by Berry. If you can navigate past the ring singularity, you still keep falling into new regions of space and time but possibly without being crushed or torn apart by tidal forces. Coming out the other side, the space traveler would be in a quite different region of space-time from that which he left to enter the hole—a different universe or perhaps a different part of our own Universe. For a large black hole of 1,000 or more solar masses, the forces involved need not be so extreme as to cause death or wreck the space ship, because the bigger a black hole is, the easier it is to get into. Yet it would be a very strange experience, with time no longer flowing in its earthly sense during the journey. To quote Taylor again, "The psychological problems would be as great as the gravitational ones." In principle, as he also says, the problem is already solved. If we had a 1,000 solar-mass rotating black hole, we could soon solve the technological problem of building a spaceship capable of getting through it. The Bacon Foundation might then have some trouble deciding who gets the prize.

How do the prize givers determine what the correct solution is? As far as I can see, he can never show this is a correct solution because no information can come out from the black hole as to what's happening to people who've fallen in. And so we have this rather embarrassing situation, possibly, of other people who've submitted attempted solutions, who'd claim that theirs are as good as the one that has been given the prize. And it seems to me that the only way to show that there is a correct solution is to make all the candidates, together with the prize giver, to fall into the black hole; those who have survived will say yes, they had the right solution, and none of us will know which was the correct answer.[6]

The point is that you cannot determine in advance when and where in space-time your journey through the black hole will end. There is no way you can get back to claim the prize. Diving back into the hole from the other side will not bring you home but will give you another mystery trip to yet another part of space-time. Taylor makes the hazards clear.

> Anybody who wishes to carry out an actual test of what has been suggested as a solution . . . what sort of orbit you should try and aim for, what angle you go in . . . should be very cautious, because it might be a pretty disastrous situation after you've got through that rotating black hole—it may not be a world you want to live in.[7]

That is not so different from what faced early explorers on Earth, and if, somehow, a way back could be found, by trial and error or otherwise, the discovery of rotating black holes—naked singularities—could lead to exploration of the Universe or the universes. If diving into a certain black hole at a certain angle and with a certain speed always brings the traveler out in the same place, and if he can then find another hole through which a dive at a certain angle and speed takes him home again, real space-time travel could be possible. In speculative fantasy stories, such as Philip Farmer's "World of Tiers" series,[8] a gate through space-time into another universe is a common device. Just how you would catch a 1,000-solar-mass rotating black hole and tame it I shall leave, as does Berry, to the technologists, for when it seems as if even speculative fantasy, let alone science fiction, is no more fantastic than the possibilities implicit in modern cosmological ideas, the time has come to pause for breath.

The best answer to the question, why should a white hole gush? is, it seems, the simplest: why not? Before looking at how our Universe might fit into a greater and more complex scheme of things, with the aid of multiple connections or wormholes, it is appropriate to look at how our planet fits into the Universe itself, using ideas that might once have seemed fantastic but now look, in comparison with much of the above, almost humdrum.

6

THE EARTH AND
THE UNIVERSE

In Chapter 4 we saw how intimately our Solar System and the Earth are related to the spiral structure of our Galaxy, and I speculated on the way this spiral structure may itself be related to the existence of a galactic gusher at the nucleus of our Galaxy. The discussion can now be taken an important step further. Roger Penrose mentions his feelings of unease regarding the possible existence of white holes:

> The reason is basically this. Once a black hole is formed *there is apparently no means of destroying it*. It is created violently, but then it settles down and sits around forever—or until the universe re-collapses at the end of time. Now a white hole—the time reverse of a black hole—would have had to have *been* there since the beginning of time—tamely and invisibly biding its time before making its presence known to us. Then, when its moment arrives, it explodes into ordinary matter.[1]

The first line of italics is mine, emphasizing that when those words were written the Hawking concept of black holes evaporating and even exploding had not activated interest among relativists. In the light of Hawking's work, we must now consider the possibility of primeval black holes tamely biding their time before exploding into ordinary matter. However, even without black-hole explosions, Penrose's objections are a matter of personal taste, not fundamental physics or mathematics. White holes seem to me to provide a balance with black holes and to offer a symmetrical view of the Universe. I find the prospect of white holes exploding forth as cosmic gushers—in small imitation of the established behavior of the Universe—more appealing than the disappearance of matter into an indestructible black hole. I cannot stress too much that no one has ever seen a black hole collapse or found any hard evidence of violent collapse in the Universe. Contrariwise, we *can* see the entire Universe expanding as a cosmic gusher and we do see violent outbursts from energetic galaxies and quasars. Penrose doesn't like that, saying, "We are stuck with the Big Bang and that also seems untidy," but he cannot deny that the Universe expands.

When Penrose discusses the implications of a naked singularity rotating at the center of our Galaxy, then, he at least is thinking very much in terms of a singularity formed by collapse:

> Suppose that some form of large rapidly rotating mass at one time collected at the center of our galaxy and that this mass approached a regime at which the effects of general relativity dominated . . .

---

if the rotation remains too great, the solution will
not in fact describe a black hole. Instead the matter
would contract down until a naked singularity is
revealed in a ring around the equatorial region.

This kind of naked singularity has the curious property
that it can only influence outside events in the equatorial
plane of the ring—it is only naked when viewed from
that plane. Any influence from the singularity would be
beamed in the plane, and, as Penrose speculates, there
might be a tie-up between the beaming plane and the plane
of our Galaxy in which the spiral arms lie. The main
snag with this idea of such a naked singularity forming
by collapse is, as we have seen, the time-scale involved
in accumulating material in this way in an expanding
universe. It is all very well to say the material may have
collected at one time, but when? There just has not been
time enough in the Universe in which we live. Could
there be a naked singularity at the galactic center, produced by a white hole and beaming its influence in a
plane in the same way? It might be necessary on such a
model to explain the large angular momentum in an
expanding system by a fission process in which two embryonic galactic nuclei split away, with equal and opposite spin, from some larger mass, but there seems to be
no other difficulty in explaining the structure of the Milky
Way, and even that one difficulty is less than the over-

whelming time-scale problem of any model involving collapse. I share Penrose's views about naked singularities in one respect—they provide exciting new possibilities for physics and that is not a prospect to cause alarm. We do not yet have a theory to cope with the problems of space-time singularities, but, like Penrose, I think that such a theory will be found. He writes:

> In any case, we have for some time been confronted by the profound theoretical problems of the Big Bang singularity, and a theory is needed to cope with this. Would it not be far more exciting if in addition there were other space-time singularities accessible to view *now* which could supply observational means of testing such a new theory? Perhaps then the mysteries of the initial creation could be more readily comprehended.[2]

Links of Influence

On the universal scale of things, relating the nature of our home planet to the spiral structure of the Galaxy and the cosmic gusher at its center is unimpressive. Yet, according to many cosmologists, there are deep and fundamental links between Earth and the overall large-scale structure of the Universe. Speculation about the way the Earth might be influenced by celestial events began when man first looked to the sky and stars and pondered on their relation to events on the ground. Astrologers have their own ideas about how such influences work and their results. For us, the story begins with Newton.

The question that Newton set out to answer concerns the establishment of an absolute frame of reference, to enable us to say definitively that, for example, the Earth orbits the Sun and the Sun does not orbit the Earth. This question is intimately related to the association of acceleration with force and to the idea that any body not acted upon by an external force stays at rest or is in uniform motion in a straight line. Thus, the curved path of the Earth's orbit around the Sun is explained by the force of the Sun's gravity on the Earth. But what about the apparent daily movement of the stars around the Earth? Obviously, the Earth is spinning; no one today can seriously claim that the Earth is at rest while the entire Universe rotates around it. Newton's laws of motion predict that a spinning body will have a bulging equator and flattened poles, as does the Earth. The rotation of the Earth relative to the distant stars, or, more accurately, remote galaxies, produces this effect, but how does the Earth "know" about the average distribution of all the rest of the material in the Universe?

In Newton's time, the point was put by Bishop Berkeley, in connection with what is now a well-known experiment involving a bucket of water. The idea of the experiment is that if a bucket of water is rotated by hanging it by the handle from a cord and giving it a good spin, friction between the bucket and the water will cause the water to spin. The water will rise up the sides of the bucket to form a concave surface. Stop the bucket suddenly and the water will continue to rotate and it will still form a concave surface until friction stops its motion. Bishop Berkeley's view was that if the stars are rotating relative to the water surface, then the surface is curved, and he concluded that the stars or, as we would now say, the average matter distribution in the Universe cause the physical effects associated with rotation. This concept is crucial to much of modern cosmological thought, and it is unfortunate that Bishop Berkeley was so far ahead of his time that his name was almost forgotten. His ideas were generally credited to Ernst Mach, who tidied them up one-and-a-half centuries later and was immortalized by Einstein, who called the concept Mach's principle. The name has stuck, but today Bishop Berkeley, having gained his rightful place in cosmological history, is acknowledged as the originator of Mach's principle.

The Theory of General Relativity is, in large measure, Einstein's attempt to incorporate Mach's principle into a gravitational view of the Universe, with gravity as the underlying force by which the total mass of the Universe influences local events. The behavior of falling bodies, orbiting satellites, swinging pendulums, and buckets of water are but a few examples of the influence of the Universe on our daily lives. According to some theorists, there may be more detailed influences at work, influences which have not been explained as satisfactorily as General Relativity explains the gravitational influences.

The idea that there may be a fundamental link between atomic and elementary particle processes and the overall structure of the Universe comes from a comparison of some of the constants of physics and cosmology. The idea goes back to the thirties, when speculations were published by the great physicist, Paul Dirac, whose name at least will be familiar since it has been taken up by several science-fiction writers describing pseudoscientific space drives.[3]

Dirac's theory of large numbers rests on the construction of two large, dimensionless numbers—one from atomic physics and one from cosmology. The idea behind this construction is that, in physics, it is often possible to produce dimensionless equations independent of the units of measurement chosen, and these usually have important physical significance. For example, we may say that one person is twice as old as another, and that would be true whether we measure age in years, days, months, or whatever. When describing the two people, that single fact would be a more valuable piece of information than knowing what units are used to measure their ages in. In atomic physics, what seems to be a fundamental constant emerges when we compare the electric force acting between a proton and an electron and the gravitational force between the same pair of particles. The first is proportional to the product of the charges and to the inverse of the square of the distance between them; the second is proportional to the product of their masses and to the inverse of the square of the distance between them. The ratio of the two forces, the force constant, is a dimensionless number which has the large, even by astronomical standards, value of 2.3×10^{39}. Our experience of dimensionless numbers suggests that this figure means something important—but what?

Dirac's second number is equally large, almost exactly so, and that is what makes the pair remarkable. Taking the age of the Universe in terms of a fundamental unit of time, the time needed for light to cross the tiny distance occupied by an atom, Dirac arrives at a number close to 10^{39}, and by dividing the mass of the Universe by the mass of a hydrogen atom, cosmologists have argued that the total number of particles in the observable Universe is approximately 10^{78}, which is the square of 10^{39}. It doesn't matter what multiple of 10^{39} is used; they are not accurate enough for that to be meaningful. But all agree to within less than one multiple of ten, in a coincidence that stretches across thirty-nine multiples of ten. If you find it difficult to grasp the meaning of such numbers, you are not alone; Jagjit Singh[4] mentions the legend of a king who was inveigled into promising an advisor a reward made up of wheat which would be counted by placing one grain on the first square of a chessboard, two on the second, four on the third, and so on. The total from the sixty-four squares would be about two-thousand times the amount of wheat produced in the world each year today; and that number only involves twenty multiples of ten, a tiny fraction of one of Dirac's large numbers.

A remarkable aspect of this work is that after Dirac's first thoughts on the subject were published in the thirties, forty years elapsed before he rounded the ideas off and completed his theory of large numbers in papers published in the seventies. This theory certainly produces a striking view of the Universe, since its continued expansion and its increasing age imply that if the agreement between these large numbers today is not just a coincidence then they must all be increasing together as the Universe expands so that even the fundamental force constant of atomic physics is actually a variable. There is one aspect to the complete theory which will be familiar to those who have come across other alternatives to Einstein's theory. Once again, it adds a two-component structure to the metric of space-time. This time one component enters through Einstein's equations, which remain valid in the Dirac universe, and the other affects what we can actually measure in the laboratory when investigating atomic behavior. According to Dirac, the variation in the force constant is due to a change in the constant of gravity, which enters into the gravitational part of the calculation of the force constant, so that the gravity constant G decreases as the age of the universe t increases.

The other figure to be juggled is that magic number for the number of particles in the observable Universe. According to Dirac, it must increase in proportion to t^2 and we are back in the Steady State scenario. Dirac offers two versions of the theory, one with the creation of matter occurring uniformly through space, and the other bringing new matter into the model universe in concentrated lumps close by existing masses, a picture superficially reminiscent of cosmic gushers. Dirac prefers the first version of the theory, however, because of the implications of new material appearing in the fabric of the rocks of the Earth, a process which would produce detectable changes in the rocks. Furthermore, in an almost heretical rejection of the expansion of the Universe, Dirac suggests that the red shift of distant galaxies is only a result of the change in the constant of gravity as the Universe has aged. Long ago, when light from distant galaxies set out, G was larger, says Dirac, and this would produce a red shift effect like the effect of a Doppler shift in an expanding universe. It is hardly surprising that this remarkable cosmology is, in the words of Dr. Paul Davies, "unpalatable for most modern cosmologists." Yet, as Davies also says, these ideas "are the product of a lively imagination, challenging the fundamental principles on which modern theories of astronomy, cosmology, and physics are founded. Coming from a physicist of Dirac's stature, that is at the very least thought provoking."[5]

Does Gravity Weaken?

Another physicist, Fred Hoyle, of lesser stature but more well known today than Dirac, recently has offered a theory of the Universe closely echoing some of Dirac's ideas.[6] Hoyle and Narlikar, his longtime colleague, offered their interpretation of some puzzling aspects of observed red shifts in an article in *Nature*[7] at the beginning of the seventies. They were especially concerned with the discrepancy between the red shifts of apparently physically linked objects of the kind thoroughly investigated by Arp. They resolved this by allowing for the effects of a gravitational constant that increases with time rather like the behavior of Dirac's model, but which also influences the actual masses of particles through a mass field. This represents an attempt to put into a mathematical form the ideas underlying Mach's principle. If it is relevant to the real Universe, all this would have profound effects on stars and planets, and Hoyle and Narlikar spell out what some of those effects are. According to this theory, stars would have been much brighter long ago, when they would have needed more heat to hold them up against a stronger pull of gravity. Since the dependence of gravity on time is not spelled out explicitly in all these models, there is convenient scope for astrophysicists to tinker with their equations to explain any puzzles regarding their observations of the stars. It is difficult to believe, however, in view of the reasonable success of ordinary astrophysical ideas, that the Sun could have been very much hotter than those ideas suggest, at least in the not-too-distant past. As with any other fiddle factor, the numbers can be juggled to remove the problem of the absence of solar neutrinos. In the case of geophysics, however, the implications of a decreasing force of gravity are clear and should produce observable effects—unfortunately, the required effects are not observed.

If gravity did weaken steadily, there would be a constant release of pressure in the Earth's interior, allowing our planet to expand at a rate which Hoyle and Narlikar calculate as 10 km in 100 million years. As they say, "There is no possibility of this expansion being resisted by the crust, which must be cracked open repeatedly to make way for new surface material," and such pressure could also be converted into horizontal forces pushing blocks of crust aside. It is a lovely idea and would once have seemed like a godsend to proponents of the theory of continental drift, when they were hard-pressed to make their case that such drift really does occur. Unfortunately for Hoyle and Narlikar, their explanation comes too late, resolving a problem that is already resolved. Few geophysicists now question the great weight of evidence in favor of continental drift, and although some question remains about how the drift is driven, the old idea that the Earth expands no longer seems tenable in the light of the discovery that old crust seems to be destroyed in deep ocean trenches at the same rate that it is created at ocean ridges. Since the Earth's crust could not resist the effects due to decreasing G (as Hoyle and Narlikar stress), then the absence of evidence for such effects on earth suggests that G has not decreased over geological time by any significant amount. Recent photographs of Mercury, obtained by the *Mariner 10* spacecraft, cast further doubt on the idea. If one planet had expanded as *G* decreased, then so should the others, but some of the most interesting geological features on Mercury seem to be the product of compression forces— if anything, Mercury has contracted since it formed. That is reasonable enough for a cooling, solidifying small planet, but once again, it does not seem generally true that all the planets have contracted, as they might have if *G* had been increasing since the formation of the Solar System, and this applies especially to the Earth.

It also seems highly unlikely that *G* has increased significantly since the Earth's crust solidified. Hoyle, however, has continued to develop this kind of idea, but in the opposite direction—away from Earth and toward the Big Bang.

Static and Variable

Hoyle's approach depends on the Machian idea that mass itself is the result of the effects of a field produced by all the other matter in the Universe. The mass field can vary from place to place and, more significantly, from time to time, so that masses may vary in Hoyle's model universe in line with the kind of changes suggested by Dirac. Yet Hoyle does more than offer an explanation of the large numbers coincidence—he does away with the physical singularity of the Big Bang by looking at his model universe differently from the usual cosmological views. The point is that, with a variable mass field, he is allowed to apply a neat mathematical trick, called a conformal transformation, to the problem; this amounts to changing the scale of measurement at different instants of time and is an accepted way of looking at some problems involving physical effects, such as electromagnetic radiation, but usually not mass, since mass is not generally taken as a variable and would vary under a conformal transformation of the kind Hoyle needs. By allowing a variable mass field, Hoyle is able to change the geometry of his model universe, reforming it so that the dramatically shrunken space in the vicinity of the Big Bang is stretched out again. The expansion of the universe is converted into the effects of increasing mass, and, as he puts it, "The usual mysteries concerning the so-called origin of the universe begin now to dissolve." If, in Hoyle's system, we choose to set the mass of each particle as constant, then the ordinary cosmology of General Relativity with an expanding universe appears from the equations, complete with the singularity of the Big Bang. Hoyle's version, a static universe with varying mass, avoids this worrisome physical singularity and introduces a different kind of singularity, a merely mathematical one that is easy to understand if you can accept the basic principle involved, the variation of mass.

According to Hoyle, the time generally regarded as the instant of creation should be seen as a time when the masses of particles just happened to go to zero. There is no problem in looking even farther back in time, past what would be the beginning of the universe in a Big Bang model. On the other side of the line, where masses are zero, we would find regions of the universe in which masses are negative; beyond them would be more regions of positive mass, and so on. We could never observe the next-door, negative mass section of such a universe, because near the zero mass boundary starlight from the other side would be very strongly blurred by interactions with the zero mass particles—but this blurred radiation would filter into the observable part of the universe as the cosmic microwave background radiation. It may seem a pity that such a neat idea should turn up in an otherwise rather odd picture of the cosmos. It is, however, quite permissible to transform Hoyle's model back into one with constant mass when the negative mass regions become regions in which the universe is collapsing instead of expanding, and the region next door becomes a previous cycle of the universe in which the singularity of the Big Bang was produced by a phase of collapse. It is even possible to explain the cosmic background radiation as scrambled starlight from the previous cycle after it has passed through the fireball of the Big Bang. First, though, we should be quite clear about the problems with models of the Universe like those of Hoyle and Dirac—problems every bit as important as the problem of the Big Bang in conventional cosmologies.

That the Earth shows no evidence of a significant change in mass or of G since the crust solidified has already been mentioned, but it is worth emphasizing. This is a rare occasion when cosmological ideas ought, in principle, to be testable through measurements and observations made by using the Earth itself as a laboratory. It's one thing to theorize a special effect in the light from distant galaxies and, if it is not observed, blame the deficiencies of the telescopes or the effect of intergalactic dust blocking our view, or whatever. It's quite another thing to look for and fail to find evidence in the very rocks beneath our feet.

If it was a surprise to find Einstein building static models of the Universe early in this century, in blatant disregard of Olbers' paradox, it is even more of a surprise to find Hoyle doing the same today, when it has been fashionable for some time to at least pay lip service to Olbers. The red shift effect of variable mass, of course, can be used to remove some of the force from the paradox by weakening the radiation spreading across the universe, but if the model universe really is infinite, with a succession of positive and negative mass zones stretching away forever, then the accumulated starlight which filters in from next door will not be at a mere 2.7 degrees, it will be exceedingly hot. If one sector produces a background of this kind and passes it on to the next, then that sector produces its own contribution to the background, plus the previous contribution, and so on. In an infinite universe the infinite sum of all these small contributions would be a blaze of light in the sky.

Small and Large

The Dirac model, which proposes the creation of matter, is even worse from the point of view of simple physical intuition, since it poses two unpleasant problems. First, it still has an origin—the time when the static, nonexpanding model universe was empty, at $t = 0$ and when the number of particles must also have been 0. This is as much of a puzzle as the Big Bang; worse is the puzzle of why we should happen to be living in such an empty part of space-time. If the universe in Dirac's model should continue indefinitely with increasing age (t increasing), then the number of particles should increase, with more and more mass being created to fill up a nonexpanding universe. Perhaps, as in Hoyle's model, the disappearance of matter at $t = 0$ can be extended to a situation with negative matter at earlier times, but why should we be living in a very unusual state of the universe? Obviously the Milky Way and our Solar System must exist somewhere in space-time. In the simplest interpretation of Dirac's model, the universe should spend only a few tens- or hundreds-of-thousands-of-millions of years warming up and should then spend a literally infinite time jam-packed with material and radiation, making the situation we see about us a very temporary passing phase. In simple physical terms, leaving aside the magic of any coincidences of large numbers, a static universe with matter creation is very much the worst of both worlds. It is tempting to believe that the agreement of those large numbers with one another is more than a coincidence, but it is very hard to accept that we have found the reason for the agreement.

So where does this leave the relationship between the Earth and the Universe? Are there any real links between microphysics and macrophysics? Almost certainly, the answer is yes, but there is a long way to go before those links are thoroughly understood. First, of course, if everything in the Universe has come from the fireball of a Big Bang, then the nature of every particle in the Universe indeed is governed by fundamental processes that operated at the beginning. If the Big Bang idea is right, and it looks far and away the best bet, then at one time the atoms of our bodies and everything else around us were in intimate contact with the atoms we can now see through giant telescopes in the distant reaches of space. The various contributors to *High Energy Astrophysics and Its Relation to Elementary Particle Physics*[8] have tried to come to grips with the nature of the links between small and large with some success but nothing as yet of major significance. One of the fundamental questions being investigated is the nature of the so-called arrow of time, which is defined by the expansion of the Universe, aging processes, and the general tendency of things to run down in a statistical sense, that is, the increase of entropy. This effort is worth singling out from the sometimes confusing pool of work done on links between fundamental particle processes and fundamental cosmological processes because of its particular importance to the oscillating universe models, which provide one of the most pleasing views of the Universe.

A. Aharony and Y. Ne'eman are among the workers who have pondered these links, and they also have an interest in the white-hole interpretation of violent astrophysical events—Ne'eman was one of the first to suggest this interpretation, which he termed a "lagging core model." Using the crucial evidence that some interactions involving the elementary particles called kaons are not time reversible, they have now built up a picture of the links between microscopic and macroscopic arrows of time. This is in line with our everyday commonsense experience that time does move in a certain direction, but quite unlike the situation in classical mechanics, where as far as the equations of motion are concerned, there is no reason why, for example, a collision and recoil involving a pair of billiard balls should occur in one direction of time or the other. A film of such a collision run backward would look quite normal as long as we did not see the player who had given the cue ball its initial velocity. The violation of this kind of time-reversal symmetry in the decay of a neutral kaon establishes conclusively the existence of a microscopic arrow of time, since if all elementary particle interactions were time symmetric there would be no way for such particles to know which way time is flowing. The links between this arrow of time and the universal, or cosmological, arrow of time are investigated by looking at how kaons ought to behave in a collapsing universe, or, if you like, in an oscillating universe where the cosmological arrow of time reverses in some sense at the singularity. It turns out that the time-reversed picture of the significant interactions is in line with the time-reversed picture of the model universe. Because these interactions do *not* look exactly the same when the film is run backward, there will be different laws of physics operating in a collapsing universe, or in the collapsing phase of an oscillating universe, compared with the physical laws we know on Earth today.

The fact that the Universe expands—that the Universe itself is a cosmic gusher or white hole—is therefore seen to be absolutely crucial in determining the laws of physics that apply to us. At last, a fusion between cosmology and physics is beginning to develop in mathematical form an account of the links between great and small that are implicit in Mach's principle, and, in this sense, perhaps a new physics is at hand. Still, this is not likely to be a revolutionary development that sweeps away the foundations of physics as we know it, but rather a logical progression, a step forward and beyond ordinary physics that not only keeps ordinary physics as the practical tool for us to use in most situations but should explain the basis of the old physics in terms of the new. This basis depends upon the very structure of the Universe; it is where the coincidence of Dirac's large numbers may at last be explained in a satisfactory manner.

Part III
Where Are We Going?

7

SYMMETRY
IN THE UNIVERSE
1: A Two-sided Balloon?

It looks as if we cannot get away from the reality of the singularity in which the Universe was created. As W. H. McCrea has said, "The history of the universe inferred from big-bang theory is self-consistent in so many unexpected ways that it can scarcely be illusory." One unsatisfactory feature of Big Bang cosmologies in general remains, and that is their inherent lack of symmetry. If the Universe appeared from a unique white-hole event and will expand indefinitely as time goes by, then we have an asymmetric situation in time—the arrow of time always points the same way, entropy increases, and the Universe ages forever. There is also an important question concerning the asymmetry of matter—are all the stars and galaxies made of the same kind of matter that we are—the odd bits left over from annihilations in the cosmic fireball—or is there an equal quantity of antimatter separated out in the form of some of the galaxies we can see? Or, is there a vast antimatter region of the Universe beyond the range of our telescopes and other detectors? The difficulty in getting a grasp on such questions and in deciding whether or not they are worth asking stems partly from the fact that we are well adapted to our Universe or we wouldn't be here at all. Naturally, the environment to which we are adapted seems normal; an inhabitant of the tropics might wonder why anyone would choose to live in northern Europe, while a Laplander might regard the tropics with great distaste. Maybe our Universe only looks natural because it is what we are used to, but the argument can be turned on its head. We can say, not that life is well adapted to the Universe, but that our Universe is an ideal place for life to have emerged. This has brought cosmologists into the borderland between their discipline and philosophy. The idea has been mooted that it might be possible for a whole variety of universes to exist, either in some way simultaneously or in some sense following each other in time, and that we happen to live in the kind of universe we see around us just because it is the best kind for the evolution of life. In that picture, most universes are devoid of life and go through their evolutionary courses unobserved.

Cosmologist Paul Davies has summed up the situation succinctly; beginning with the question, how special is the Universe? He has suggested that "The Universe has been created in a singularly convenient form for the presence of intelligent life." The numbers game familiar from Dirac's studies comes in here again. If the coupling constant of the strong interaction of physics, which is so

important in determining the rate of nuclear reactions, were even a few percent bigger, then most of the hydrogen in the Universe would have been converted into heavier elements in the fireball of the Big Bang. With little hydrogen around, stable stars like the Sun could not exist, since they depend on the nuclear burning of hydrogen fuel. There is an intriguing argument that since the ratio of the electrical and gravitational forces between electron and proton (Dirac's first large number) is critical in fixing the time it takes for a star to evolve, which will be the time it has also taken for the highest forms of life to evolve, then it should be no surprise that this number is roughly comparable to the age of the Universe in atomic units (Dirac's second large number). Recently various cosmologists have investigated the evolution of universes that start out from a Big Bang situation different from our own, either inhomogeneously or nonisotropically, and they have found persuasive evidence that such universes develop very quickly into homogeneous, isotropic states like our own. Even so, homogeneous and isotropic universes could exist, as far as we know, with different laws of physics from those we know and love. And, as Davies has stressed, "the adoption of the philosophy that the existence of life imposes severe constraints on the structure of the Universe" does not imply "a 'purpose-built' world with men as the end product." There may indeed be a whole ensemble of universes with a wide range of properties, in most of which life is impossible because the special conditions that we guess are necessary for life and that exist in our own Universe are not generally met. In only a few universes can life evolve to become aware of its surroundings, and those universes must be quite like ours. "In a nutshell," says Davies, "the world we live in is the world we live in." But where are the other universes?

Universal Cycles

One possibility is that the Universe is cyclic. The expansion phase may be followed by collapse back into the fireball followed by a re-expansion, in which different laws of physics may apply. Such cycles could continue indefinitely, producing an indefinite succession of different universes, with only rare cycles permitting life to evolve. It is difficult to say much more about such bouncing universes, but one detailed theory deserves special mention and will be treated fully in the next chapter. Meanwhile, there is another way to produce a multiplicity of universes, one which is an old favorite from science fiction, the concept of parallel universes. The idea of the Universe constantly splitting to follow different paths is an old one in science fiction; a quarter of a century ago Clifford Simak described a variation on the theme in terms of discrete time intervals [that]:

> there might be more worlds than one, that there might be a world a second ahead of ours and one a second behind ours and another a second behind that and still another and another and another, a long string of worlds whirling one behind the other, like men walking in the snow, one man putting his foot into the other's track and the one behind him putting his foot in the same track and so on down the line.
>
> An endless chain of worlds, one behind the other. A ring around the Sun.[1]

The point of that story was that it might be possible to jump from one world to another around the ring, but science has not as yet caught up with science fiction. H. Beam Piper made parallel universes his own with a series of stories going back to the forties and extending into the sixties, right up to his untimely death. From *Gunpowder God,* here is a 1964 version of the theory:

> Twelve thousand years ago, facing extinction on an exhausted planet, the First Level race had discovered the existence of a second, lateral dimension of time, and a means of physical transposition to and from the worlds of alternate probability parallel to their own. . . .

> Fourth Level was the big one. The others had devolved from low-probability genetic accidents; Fourth had been the maximum probability. It was divided into many sectors and subsectors, on most of which civilization had first appeared in the Nile and Tigris-Euphrates valleys. . . .[2]

Again, we don't have the means of physical transposition, but compare those words with Paul Davies' comments of 1974:

> It is well known that quantum theory cannot predict precisely the outcome of any realistic experiment, but at best can only give the relative probabilities of the outcomes. Conventionally, it is supposed that the real world selects from all the choices one particular result at random, but Everett has developed a theory in which all possible quantum alternatives

presented are in fact realized, by the entire world splitting continuously into a stupendous number of parallel worlds. Once again, only a small subset of such worlds would permit the existence of life.[3]

Even more outrageous ideas emerge when we try applying these quantum mechanical ideas to the Big Bang itself. Grand speculations are, of course, nothing new, and, as long ago as the nineteenth century, Boltzman, puzzling over the curious fact that the Universe is not in thermodynamic equilibrium, suggested that maybe it is usually in equilibrium but occasionally undergoes a vast convulsion—a universal hiccup—in which non-equilibrium conditions reign temporarily. The picture is rather like that of the cyclic theory—we are only here to see the present hiccup because it is the right kind of convulsion to allow the formation of life. But what would the normal equilibrium be like? The smoothest equilibrium of all must be an empty vacuum, and Edward P. Tryon of the City University of New York has proposed that the entire Universe as we know it may be simply a quantum fluctuation from a normal universal vacuum. This model is, he suggests, "the simplest and most appealing imaginable—namely, that our Universe is a fluctuation of the vacuum, where vacuum fluctuation is to be understood in the sense of quantum field theory."

The relevant point taken from that theory and adopted by Tryon is, essentially, that if something can happen, it will—eventually. Provided all the necessary conservation laws are obeyed (conservation of mass, energy, and so on) within the framework of quantum mechanics and the uncertainty principle, then it is possible, for example, for an electron, a positron, and a photon to emerge occasionally and spontaneously from a perfect vacuum. When this happens, the three particles exist for a brief time and then they annihilate each other, leaving no trace behind. Although energy conservation is violated, this is only for a very brief time, Δt, allowed by the uncertainty relation that tells us that we cannot measure energy and time-interval any more accurately than is allowed by the relation

$$\Delta E \, \Delta t = h$$

where h is Planck's constant. Planck's constant is, to be sure, rather small at 6.62620×10^{-27} erg sec, but it's the principle of the thing that matters, and this kind of vacuum fluctuation is quite commonplace in quantum field theory. The important point is that the more accurately energy is conserved, the longer is the time-interval allowed for the fluctuation; in principle, if energy were exactly conserved ($\Delta E = 0$) then Δt could be infinite, and even with a very small value of ΔE (small, that is, compared with h) we could have a respectably large Δt. Tryon goes all the way and suggests that the entire Universe is a quantum fluctuation of this kind—in other words, Δt is at least the age of the Universe and probably substantially bigger since the Universe shows no signs of disappearing without a trace just yet. The corollary is that ΔE must be very small indeed, so that for all practical purposes, the total energy of the Universe is zero. Tryon suggests how this could be.

The enormous amount of mass energy in the Universe, argues Tryon, is very nearly canceled out by the enormous amount of negative gravitational energy it possesses. This is another way of saying that the expansion rate of the Universe is very close to the critical boundary between open models, which expand forever, and closed models, which must one day collapse back into the fireball state. The argument holds exactly, it seems, for any closed universe:

> Suppose the Universe were closed. Then it would be topologically impossible for any gravitational flux lines to escape. If the Universe were viewed from the outside, by a viewer in some larger space in which the Universe were imbedded, the absence of gravitational flux would imply that the system had zero energy. Hence any closed universe has zero energy.[4]

So the Universe could be just a passing flicker in the vacuum of some greater emptiness—hardly something to give us a feeling of importance, but Tryon can go one step better still in indicating the insignificance of man and his Universe. Such a fluctuation is not even very likely, he points out, but if there is any probability of its happening at all, then it will happen sometime:

> . . . any universe in which sentient beings find themselves is necessarily hospitable to sentient beings. I do not claim that universes like ours occur frequently, merely that the expected frequency is nonzero. Vacuum fluctuations on the scale of our Universe are probably quite rare. The logic of the situation dictates, however, that observers always find themselves in universes capable of generating life, and such universes are impressively large. (We could not have seen this Universe if its expansion-

contraction time had been less than the 10^{10} yr required for *Homo sapiens* to evolve.)[5]

The Matter of Antimatter

The implication of all this is that the Universe must have the overall quantum numbers appropriate for the vacuum, including not just zero total energy but also equal quantities of matter and antimatter, which will be mutually annihilated when the re-collapse, which is inevitable in Tryon's model, eventually occurs. This is a satisfactory state of symmetry in many ways, but is there any evidence that there is a symmetrical distribution of matter and antimatter in the Universe? Certainly, if there were any way of proving that there is more matter than antimatter around, then Tryon's speculation would have to be thrown out; but although the antimatter debate has quieted in recent years, following some intense discussions in the fifties, the question has yet to be resolved.

Twenty years ago, excitement about antimatter was stirred by the discovery of violent events in the Universe. Even before quasars were discovered, astrophysics was having difficulty explaining the energies involved in radio galaxies. Those were the days when it was speculated that colliding galaxies might provide the necessary energy, with a soupçon of matter/antimatter annihilation as well. Now we know there are far too many radio galaxies to be explained in terms of galactic collisions, which are rare events; as more and more energetic sources have been discovered, there has been an increasing need to explain their energetic powerhouses, but at the same time, antimatter has looked less and less plausible as the explanation. Even in 1958, Burbidge and Hoyle were able to show convincingly that in our own Galaxy, "the ratio of antimatter to ordinary matter in our interstellar gas cannot possibly be more than one part in ten million, spread thinly," and it is equally unlikely that other galaxies contain a mixture of antimatter and matter. How then could matter/antimatter annihilation explain the explosion of a galaxy into the Seyfert or quasar state? Perhaps separate galaxies, or separate clusters of galaxies, could be respectively matter and antimatter, but, if so, how did the two kinds of material become separated during the early stages of the Big Bang?

If an evolutionary Big Bang universe started out with equal amounts of matter and antimatter, as symmetry arguments suggest, then the atoms and anti-atoms must have become separated, and the only way that that might happen is if anti-atoms also have antigravity, so that they are repelled from normal matter. Burbidge and Hoyle found this idea repulsive in more ways than one, saying, "It is upon this rock that the antimatter ideas have foundered. For the idea of antigravity cannot be accepted without destroying the basic principles of the general theory of relativity." That did not stop Hoyle (with Narlikar) from introducing a version of antigravity in his C-field theory of a Steady State universe in the sixties, and critics of that theory might well be amused by the further comment he made in the 1958 article with Burbidge:

> The successes of the relativity theory are so great that most scientists are not prepared at the present

time to consider with equanimity the very considerable upheaval that would come if it had to be
abandoned or drastically modified.[6]

Perhaps observations of quasars provide the necessary indication that such an upheaval must now be con-
templated; even so, there is no good reason to believe
that antimatter possesses antigravity, and there is no
observational evidence that antimatter exists in the Universe in any great quantity. This looks bleak for Tryon's
theory, but perhaps something might be salvaged by
incorporating the ideas of M. Goldhaber, put forward
in 1956, into a new kind of symmetrical model of the
Universe. This model depends on the speculation that
the primeval fireball—the primeval atom, cosmic egg,
or, in Isaac Asimov's shorthand, cosmeg—of the Universe divided immediately into two parts after formation, one matter and one antimatter, which separated in
some unspecified way to become two related universes,
one of matter and one of antimatter, each unobservable
from the other. This would salvage all the symmetry
implicit in our present understanding of the behavior of
elementary particles, and there is even a way of imagining where the antimatter universe, the counterpart of
our own material world, might be.

Our Counterpart Under the Skin

The already used analogy of the expanding Universe
being like the surface of an expanding balloon can give
a new insight to the matter/antimatter problem. In that,
clusters of galaxies are imagined as dots on the outer

surface of the balloon, while the rubber of the balloon is the fabric of space. Expanding the balloon and stretching the fabric moves the dots farther apart. The model is closed; it has no boundaries and a finite area, which is the surface of the spherical balloon. Though I like the oft-used analogy, I've always wondered what the equivalent in the real Universe of the inside of the balloon might be. Imagine dots on the inside skin as well, sharing the same fabric of space in some way but not communicating directly with the dots painted on the outside. If the expanding balloon started out initially from zero volume, all the dots were together in the Big Bang when the expansion started, but they very soon became separated into two families, one on the inner and one on the outer skin. Could one family be matter and the other antimatter? I see no reason why not, and by likening the Universe to a two-sided balloon we can retain the attractive material symmetry idea with none of the complications. With our new knowledge of black and white holes, we can even find a way for the two universes to communicate.

Another well-used analogy, about the way space is stressed by the gravitational field of a massive object, involves a heavy spherical object placed on a stretched rubber sheet. The rubber is stretched by the weight of the object. For a very heavy, very compact mass the sheet will be stretched so much that it will be punctured, making a hole through the fabric into new regions of space on the other side. Can we, then, imagine black and white holes as the punctures in the skin of the two-sided balloon, punctures that allow the flow of matter or antimatter between universes? If the cosmic gushers we see in quasars really are leaking antimatter into our

Universe from the other side, it's no wonder that they react so violently with their surroundings, quite apart from the pressure built up as they have squeezed through the tunnel. And our dying galaxies, falling into black holes in our Universe, may be squeezing through into the inside skin of the balloon, emerging to react with equal violence with the antimatter they find there. Perhaps eventually so much material will have been exchanged that our side will become predominately antimatter, and the other side chiefly matter; the transferred material will then settle down into new galaxies and stars, evolve, and collapse into black holes for the cycle to repeat. Such speculation has long been the very lifeblood of cosmology. Now some science-fiction writer is needed to describe the results of communication between both sides of the balloon. Isaac Asimov came close with *The Gods Themselves,* but anyone eager to improve on that in terms of the science involved needs to be quick, since science fact is very rapidly overhauling science fiction in the area of mysterious communication across barriers once believed to be impenetrable.

In the Asimov story, there is contact between universes that operate with different physical laws. The story is reminiscent of those speculations about the strength of the aforementioned strong interaction, and its characters gain energy by permitting material to leak in from a universe where the nuclear interaction is 100 times stronger than in their own.

Plutonium-186, stable in their universe, contains far too many protons, or too few neutrons, to be stable in ours with its less effective nuclear interaction. The plutonium-186, once in our Universe, begins to radiate positrons, releasing energy as it does so, and with each positron emitted, a proton within a nucleus is converted to a neutron . . . for every plutonium-186 nucleus sent to us, our Universe ends up with twenty fewer electrons.

But the donors in the other universe (Asimov terms it a para-Universe) are not altruistic. The plutonium-186 arrives because it has been exchanged for tungsten-186, which is similarly unstable over there:

> With each tungsten-186 nucleus sent into the para-Universe, twenty more electrons are added to it. The plutonium/tungsten can make its cycle endlessly . . . both sides can gain energy from what is, in effect, an Inter-Universe Electron Pump.

Problems occur when the physical laws of the two universes become mixed by the pump, so that there is a danger of the Sun exploding because of the changing value of the nuclear interaction. This is resolved by the development of a means of access to a variety of other parallel universes with a variety of other physical laws, so that a judicious admixture of weaker nuclear interaction can be leaked back in to maintain the status quo. The source of this weaker interaction in Asimov's tale is worthy of interest in the context of the nature of the Big Bang:

> Suppose, now, that we had a much less intense strong interaction than that which prevails in our Universe. In that case, huge masses of protons would have so little tendency to fuse that a very

large mass of hydrogen would be needed to support a star . . . a Universe would exist which consisted of a single star containing all the mass in that Universe . . . the anti-para-Universe I am picturing consists of what some call a cosmic egg; or "cosmeg" for short.

When the strong interaction from our Universe leaks into the cosmeg universe, nuclear fusion is triggered and Asimov's cosmeg explodes in a manner he likens to the Big Bang, suggesting mischievously that our Big Bang was caused by similar external interference. I'm sure that Asimov knows the important difference between a universe in which all the matter is located in one part of space and a *singularity,* in which space and time, as well as matter, are wrapped up into one spacetime singularity, like the singularity of space-time from which the white hole of our Universe gushed.

By linking these Asimovian ideas with the concept of a two-sided balloon, I have sneaked in an assumption which should be elucidated, even granting that we are floating up into the airy realm of speculation.

If there is a variety of parallel universes of one kind or another, the simple two-sided balloon analogy is inadequate. Now, we are contemplating a whole array of two-sided balloons; each may be a neat quantum-number-conserved entity in its own right, and be part of a set of parallel universes. It might be difficult to communicate between them, even with the aid of wormholes and space-time tunnels, but, while we are stretching our imaginations like the stretching fabric of space itself, why not picture the whole array embedded in superspace? Or how about supertime? Perhaps the succession of balloons really follows as different cycles of an oscillating Universe, each with its own physical laws. A black-hole-white-hole space-time tunnel can as readily emerge elsewhen as elsewhere; there's a nice touch Asimov missed—the cosmeg with which his heroes are tampering, incidentally triggering a pseudo Big Bang, could be the cosmeg from which our own Universe began its expansion.

Swifter Than Light

If there are problems distinguishing fact from fiction in some areas of cosmology, that is equally true of another aspect of modern physical thought, which, coincidentally, also provides another speculative means of communication across the barriers of space and time. This is the concept of tachyons, particles that, even within the framework of relativity theory, are allowed to travel faster than light—provided, that is, that they *always* travel faster than light.

In science-fiction literature, such faster-than-light particles have been used as a means by which a faster-than-light matter-transmitter can shoot messages, objects, and even copies of people between the stars as conveniently as TV is now squirted across the gulf between the continents. Yet, even this idea is humdrum compared with the serious suggestions of some physicists concerning the potential of tachyons for time travel and telepathic communication. The story began with the first claims that tachyons had been detected, made in 1974 by Roger Clay and Philip Crouch of Adelaide University in Australia.

The second biggest cliché (after $E = mc^2$) to emerge from Einstein's work on relativity is that no particle can cross the barrier of the speed of light; however, the solutions of Einstein's equations permit two families of particles to exist, one which always has a speed less than that of light, and the other which always has a speed greater than that of light. The latter are tachyons, particles for which, if they do exist, many of our normal physical laws are reversed, so that, for example, a tachyon accelerates as it *loses* energy. To slow such a particle down, energy must be added, in a manner reminiscent of the Red Queen's instruction to Alice that she would have to run as fast as she could in order to stay in one place. Even now, many physicists argue that the prediction of tachyons from relativity theory is a quirk of the mathematics, with no physical meaning, in just the same way that engineers generally discard one of the two possible solutions to a quadratic equation when designing their constructions.

If tachyons exist, they are most likely to be found in cosmic ray showers that are produced when energetic particles from space strike the top of our atmosphere, as are other exotic particles. These showers of secondary particles travel at very nearly the speed of light and can be detected at ground level. A series of 1,300 such showers which arrived near Adelaide, Australia, between February and August 1973 was analyzed by Clay and Crouch, who made the surprising discovery that, just before the arrival of each burst of radiation, their detectors picked up an extra signal. Such "precursor bursts" seem to be associated with the cosmic ray showers, but they travel ahead of them—faster than particles which are themselves moving virtually at the speed of light.

Clay and Crouch suggest that the precursors represent bursts of tachyons produced when a very energetic primary cosmic ray hits the atmosphere.

This remarkable claim is enough to justify further flights of fancy, even in the absence of additional observations to support the suggestion made by Clay and Crouch. But, first a word of caution. at about the same time in the mid-seventies, another team of cosmic ray observers claimed to have found evidence of another mysterious particle, the quark, which physicists have proposed as the fundamental building block of such elementary particles as electrons and protons. The data were difficult to interpret and have yet to be verified. Although the first press reports of these claims were, hardly surprisingly, given such headlines as "The Hunting of the Quark," the full story was that, of the three investigators concerned with this work at Leeds University, England, one thought the evidence might show the presence of quarks, one thought there could be a conventional explanation, and the third suggested the evidence implied the presence of another as yet hypothetical particle, the vector boson. What the headline writers missed was that some quarks are bosons, a situation not only to delight readers of Lewis Carroll but to emphasize the confusion that can be caused by cosmic ray showers.

With the caution that even the existence of tachyons may still be a subject for debate in the hard world of factual reality, I cannot resist the opportunity to dip a toe into the ocean of science-fiction speculation by invoking tachyons to explain a curious phenomenon of our times, the spoon bending and other activities of Uri Geller and his followers. The "tachyonic link" in this connection can be seen by looking first at Isaac Asimov's thirty-year-old tale of the remarkable properties of re-sublimated thiotimoline, a compound so partial to water that it dissolves 1.12 seconds *before* the liquid is added to it. The Asimovian explanation of this was that the carbon bonds in the molecules of thiotimoline extended not just in the usual three dimensions of space but also a short distance into the future, so that molecules dissolving in the future could drag their linked present counterparts into solution with them. A little thought shows that such a temporal bond could be achieved by a tachyonic interaction.

The standard description of the two families of particles allowed by Einstein's equations follows from the requirement that the total energy of a particle is given by

$$m_oc^2 \left(1 - (v/c)^2\right)^{1/2}$$

the key point being that taking the square root (half power) introduces two families of solutions. For zero velocity, of course, the expression reduces to our old friend, mc^2. Square roots of negative numbers, although allowed mathematically, do not usually have physical significance, and the obvious interpretation of this expression to give real total energies is that the term $(1 - (v/c)^2)$ must therefore always be positive, or at least zero, so that v is always less than or equal to c and particles never travel faster than light. But there are other ways of obtaining a real energy from the expression. We can, for example, ponder the possibilities of particles with an imaginary mass im (where i is the square root of -1); in that case, the situation is reversed, and in order to obtain a real energy we must take another square root of a negative number in order that the imaginary *i*s multiply out to −1. In other words, for imaginary masses, *v* must always *exceed c* (and is not even allowed to be equal to the speed of light) so that $(1 - (v/c)^2)$ is always negative. This is the origin of the theory of tachyons.

Suppose we allow *v* to exceed *c* while maintaining real mass *m*. Now we are taken into very strange territory—the imaginary part of the space-time continuum. Might we consider a tachyon with an imaginary mass moving through the real part of space-time at a speed greater than that of light as being in some way equivalent to a particle with real mass moving through the imaginary part of space-time on a shortcut to the future? And if so, of course, symmetry requires that the effect operate as well for time travel into the past. Tachyons can provide the link between past and future needed to bond the molecules of Asimov's thiotimoline, which are now seen as producing a continuous flux of tachyons, emitted from the present, absorbed in the future, re-emitted, and absorbed back in the present. But what can this tell us about Uri Geller?

The discussion above is intended as an exercise in speculation, and it may therefore be surprising that Jack Sarfatti, of the International Center for Theoretical Physics in Trieste, Italy, has suggested something very similar as an explanation of the way in which an observer might interact with an experiment (that is, anything around the observer) to change the quantum probability of events—choosing between the multiply branching parallel universes, if you like. If a collection of atoms in the handle of a spoon, for example, just happened to choose certain quantum states, then the spoon would bend. In a multiple universe picture, I suppose there must be a universe corresponding to any possible effect at the quantum level, and in that case we are lucky that spoon bending works here occasionally but not always. Certainly, many concepts of quantum mechanics appear quite bizarre to our minds, since we are used to the macroworld, and it is quite permissible to consider a positron moving forward in time as being equivalent to an electron moving backward in time. This is the strange territory where the theory of black-hole explosions takes root. It is also a fundamental feature of quantum theory that any observer is inextricably part of any experiment, since the very act of observing changes the situation observed—this is the underlying theme of Sarfatti's work. So, let us apply these ideas to an experiment in which a spoon-bending magician is being observed by a large theatre or TV audience.

The general mass of observers involved in such an experiment will produce an unfocused wave of tachyons, carrying, by and large, commonsense expectations about the behavior of such objects as spoons. A suitable focusing of the tachyons in line with the expectation that the spoons might bend could, if we follow Sarfatti, push over the quantum effects to produce just that situation—but when Geller produces his bent spoons it comes as a surprise to the audience. How can they have focused their tachyonic awareness to influence quantum statistics *before* the event?

The answer seems simple if tachyons can travel backward in time. The spectacular production of the bent spoons produces the wave of astonishment from the audience, releasing a flood of tachyons which travel backward in time to cause the spoons to bend just before they are produced to create the surprise. If such a process could be triggered deliberately, it would explain telepathic phenomena as the direct tachyonic communication between minds, but something as physical as spoon bending seems to require the pooled effort of many minds —except, according to John Taylor, in the case of children. This should be no surprise in the light of the above; children have more vivid imaginations than most adults, with more powerful emotions presumably releasing stronger tachyonic vibrations. Perhaps this tachyonic link even provides a clue to such mysteries as poltergeists!

So much for science fiction, for the time being at least. Perhaps tachyons could provide a means of communication with the other side of a two-sided balloon universe, or perhaps they are indeed merely a figment of mathematics. The whole business is certainly no more confusing than the story of the neutrino, where among bizarre suggestions made in desperate attempts to solve the solar neutrino puzzle, Talmadge Davis and John Ray of Clemson University in South Carolina have suggested that neutrinos might, according to their equations, exist in a state of zero momentum and zero energy, which would make them rather difficult to observe, but that, even so, they could really be present as ghost neutrinos, because there is still a mathematical wave function describing their presence:

> Ghost neutrinos appear in a natural way in general relativity . . . . Maybe these solutions do have some physical significance. It may be that these "ghost neutrinos" solutions are some type of "relic" from

the quantum theory of gravity. In some way the vacuum state in quantum gravity may be "bubbling" with virtual neutrinos and antineutrinos.[7]

That is presented as science fact. If nothing else, the whole business makes the idea of our Universe as the outer skin of some three-dimensional balloon expanding through multidimensional hyperspace seem almost homely by comparison. The two-sided balloon idea has the great merit of maintaining the symmetry of matter and antimatter overall, but it does not answer the question, where are we going? To make a stab at solving that puzzle—which has plagued man for as long as he has been aware that the future lies ahead—we need to take a look at the other side of the coin of symmetry, not just symmetry of material things but of time and of space-time.

8
SYMMETRY
IN THE UNIVERSE
2: A Repeating Bounce?

We now have a very good idea both of the origin of the Universe and of its present state, but we cannot yet quite be sure where it is going. The crucial question—is the Universe open or closed?—has not been answered, although succeeding generations of observers have pushed the limits on the known rate of expansion ever closer to the critical boundary between open and closed—the boundary corresponding to the Universe's escape velocity from itself, or to the Schwarzschild limit for the mass of the Universe. Indeed, the Universe is now seen to be so nearly in balance between the open and closed states that there is a growing suspicion among some cosmologists that this is no coincidence, that something fundamental is indicated by the possibility that our Universe may have been required to sit, if not on, then close to this critical fence. Whatever that something is, it must be extremely fundamental, since even Einstein's equations and those of other relativistic cosmologists allow a bewildering array of possible evolutionary universes.

The great revolution incorporated in relativity theory is the concept of the curvature of space-time. Why the

---

Earth moves around the Sun is seen in this picture as the result of the curvature of space-time caused by the gravity of the Sun. Instead of moving in a straight line through flat space, the planets follow the equivalent of straight lines—geodesics—in curved space, and the rubber-sheet analogy provides a graphic insight into the situation. With a massive, dense sphere in the middle of the sheet, the space-time of the sheet is curved into a dip around the sphere, and smaller spheres rolled across the sheet will be deflected by the curvature. The reality of the effect in space around the Sun has been confirmed by the bending of light from distant stars as it passes by the Sun (as observed during total eclipses) and by other effects on the orbital motion of Mercury, the closest planet to the Sun and the deepest into its gravitational potential well. But what about the curvature of the whole fabric of space-time making up the Universe itself?

If the effects of all the matter in the Universe are smoothed out to approximate a universe uniformly filled with matter—which is probably a reasonable approximation—then Einstein's equations have solutions corresponding either to negatively curved or to positively curved space-time, but not to models with curvatures independent of time. This is another way of saying that there are no static solutions to the equations, and, as we saw before, this led Einstein to invent a cosmological

constant allowing Steady State universes to exist. The later discovery of the expansion of the Universe removed both the need for the constant and its basis for existence, so those static models need not be taken seriously. The difference between those universes and the real Universe can be likened to the difference between a cylinder and a sphere; if time is the long axis of the cylinder, we have a model of a universe in which the curvature of space, around the cylinder, is uniform with time. But if we have a sphere in which the time axis corresponds to latitude and space to longitude, then both space and time are curved—in this case, with positive curvature. The alternative—negative curvature—corresponds to a saddle surface in two dimensions, or the topology of a mountain pass. And it requires no great intuitive leap to see why such negatively curved universes are open while positively curved universes are closed.

The Necessary Curvature

There is a very simple test for positive or negative curvature on a two-dimensional surface. If we draw a triangle on the surface, taking care that the sides are geodesics, which for a sphere would mean great circles, then for a negative curvature the angles add up to *less* than 180°, while for a positive curvature the angles add up to *more* than 180°. Only on a flat surface do the angles of a triangle add up to exactly 180°. In a three-dimensional universe, the question of positive or negative curvature can be solved, in theory, by the equally simple geometrical task of measuring the volume of a sphere. In flat space (Euclidean geometry), the volume increases as the cube of the radius; in negatively curved space, the increase in volume is faster than this, and in positively curved space, it is slower. Unfortunately, we need to measure a very large volume in order for such effects to be noticeable in the real Universe. It can be done by counting the numbers of galaxies we see in successively larger spheres centered on our own Galaxy, but the answer is not yet conclusive. We need more counts of fainter galaxies at greater distances to settle the issue. The consensus of opinion today is probably just on the side of continued expansion—that the Universe is negatively curved and open. If correct, this means that the white-hole explosion of the Big Bang was a unique event and that, far from going out in a blaze of glory in some eventual re-collapse into the fireball, the Universe will die away when all the stars and galaxies go out in a few billion years' time, leaving dead galaxies full of dead stars receding ever farther from one another into infinity. That is certainly an explicit and clear prediction of where we are going. It is also a very gloomy picture, but, happily, there is room for other views. An eternally expanding universe is unsatisfactory on many grounds and lacks symmetry. It may be, of course, that we are wrong to look for either symmetry or for a tidy end to the Universe, but both can be recovered within the framework of the evolutionary equations developed by Einstein and others. The optimistic view is that the possibility of our Universe being in such a situation should not be ruled out until it is proven that space-time is not positively curved. If the underlying theme of the revolutionary developments in high-energy astrophysics outlined in this book is correct, then it is a fundamental feature of the Universe that material does not disappear into one-way sinks but is constantly recycled; there is no ultimate death in a black hole, but rebirth, perhaps through a black-hole state, as a white hole. Such a Phoenix-like rebirth of the whole Universe is aptly described in Biblical terms:

> The Earth and Heaven shall become worn out as old clothes. Some day you shall fold them up and replace them in kind. (Hebrews 1:10–12)

The Evolutionary Path

So, in a spirit of optimism for the future of the Universe, I shall describe in detail the evolutionary path which seems most satisfying, with its promise of a form of eternal life, in the Universal sense. More gloomy views of the future are currently more fashionable, but fashions come and go while the Universe, so I believe, rolls on forever in an eternal cycle in which death is merely the necessary prelude to rebirth. (See figure 4.)

Apart from philosophical considerations, the oscillating model, in a form developed in the mid-seventies, provides an insight into the reason our Universe is on the edge between being open and closed. The model has been presented and developed in two scientific papers which bear the same title, "Entropy in an Oscillating Universe," one by David Park alone and the other by Park and P. T. Landsberg; their study provides some intriguing agreements between the theory and observations of the real Universe but also poses some new questions. Landsberg and Park consider a model universe in which a uniform spread of matter (gas) and a uniform spread

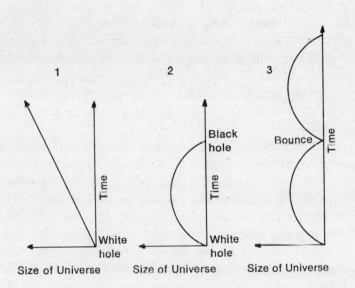

Figure 4

Models of the Universe. Model 1 expands forever; as time increases, the size of the universe increases, because it expands faster than its own escape velocity. Model 2 starts out expanding, but expands too slowly to escape from its own gravitational well. Eventually, gravity stops the expansion and then pulls all the material back into a singularity (zero size). Model 3 is a bouncing universe. Like Model 2, it collapses after the expansion phase, but it then bounces at the singularity, switching back into the expanding state.

of radiation, which is reminiscent of the cosmic background, are allowed to interact. In theoretical terms, this is a significant development incorporating features of both standard cosmology, which takes account of, and is primarily about, gravitation, and of thermodynamics and statistical mechanics, which are studies of the behavior of matter and radiation, and which do not normally concern themselves with gravitation and space-time. The result is a hybrid that the authors themselves hasten to describe as "too simple to be realistic"; but, as a first step beyond standard cosmologies of the past five decades, this simple step must be seen as a major development.

Although both the gas and the radiation are assumed to be uniformly spread throughout the universe, this is no worse an assumption than many of the standard premises of conventional cosmology, where such incidentals as galaxies are generally taken as test particles of no great account. The first important result that emerges from this incorporation of thermodynamics into cosmology is that during both the expanding and contracting phases of the oscillating model, entropy, the measure of universal disorder, increases, so that the arrow of time is constant. This is in line with what we would expect; any other result would be most puzzling. For example, if the arrow of time pointed the other way during the collapse phase, how would every particle and photon in the universe know just when to switch over into the time-reversed state? The evidence from particle physics that the preferred arrow of time in our Universe is defined both at microscopic and macroscopic levels ties in neatly with this work; in this picture, even when it is collapsing, the universe continues to get older in the same sense as in the expansion phase. The arrow of time is established once and for all in the Big Bang singularity.

Like everyone else today, Landsberg and Park do not have the mathematics to deal rigorously with singularities. For a unique Big Bang, as we have seen, cosmologists can fudge round this by considering the evolution of the Universe only since a very short time after the initial outburst from the singularity. With oscillating models, the problem rears its head repeatedly, and, in order to follow each collapse through the bounce at the singularity, Landsberg and Park are forced to cheat a little, simply reversing the collapse at a very great, but not quite singular, density, so that a universe collapsing inward at velocity *v* suddenly becomes, in their computer models, an otherwise identical universe expanding outward at the same speed. This is not entirely valid; such a treatment means that information is carried over from one cycle to the next in the computer simulations, whereas passage through a true singularity would smear out matter and radiation so much that all such information would be destroyed. Yet, as far as it goes, the model offers intriguing hints at why the Universe we live in might be in just the borderline state between being open and closed that it is.

In thermodynamics, no process is perfectly efficient— a perpetual motion machine cannot be built—and this applies even to a machine equivalent to a whole universe. If you pump up a bicycle tire, the pump gets hot because of the inefficiency of the process, and in a crudely similar way, when a cyclic universe is pumped up in the computer simulations of Landsberg and Park, it also gets hot in a sense, since its entropy continually increases. In physical terms, the result is that the collapse phase always proceeds faster than the preceding expansion, so that the oscillating universe hurtles ever more precipitously *toward* the singularity than the headlong rate at which it exploded outward *from* the singularity. As we have seen, the Landsberg-Park models switch over at the singularity simply by reversing this collapse velocity. *So every outward explosion proceeds faster than the preceding cycle.* (See figure 5.) The models are always closed—the re-collapse always takes place—but successive cycles of the oscillation start out faster and faster, expanding to greater and greater radii before they collapse in their turn, with each cycle taking longer than the one before it, and each cycle coming ever closer to the boundary between being closed and being open, without ever quite reaching it.

This behavior is, incidentally, in line with earlier calculations of oscillating universes which did not incorporate the same treatment of thermodynamics. Although it is always a feature of their models, and although we can see physically why this happens, Landsberg and Park are unable to prove mathematically that oscillating universes must always behave in this way.

So why should our Universe be very nearly unbound, but not quite? In the Landsberg-Park cosmology, successive cycles take ever longer to complete, and, in any cycle, the model spends most of its time close to the turnaround point where its outward velocity has slowed and collapse is just setting in. Early cycles were over too quickly for life as we know it to evolve, and, even in longer cycles, little time is spent in the highly dense phase near the singularity. The closeness of our Universe to the just bound state suggests that it has already been

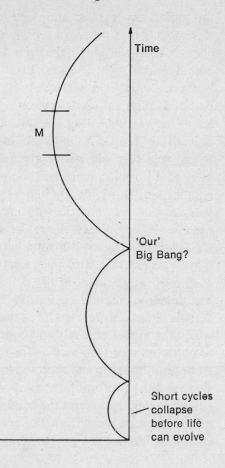

Figure 5

The Landsberg-Park model of a bouncing universe. In this model, each bounce is bigger than the one before, because each one starts out from the white hole state faster than the previous one. If our Universe is like this model, we are living at some time like the period marked M, while the universe is still expanding, but a long way from the singular state.

through many cycles and leads to the prediction, in this model, that when observational tests become good enough they will show that our Universe is indeed just bound and not just open. Pushing the model further is not really justified with the present simple assumptions, but some physical ideas remain to be explored. It might seem, for example, that the darkness of the night sky is difficult to reconcile with an ever increasing entropy from cycle to cycle, since eventually the model should give a uniform universe with matter and radiation in equilibrium. But even though matter in the model universe pours out radiation during the expansion phase, the size of the universe increases so rapidly that there is no opportunity for equilibrium between matter and radiation to be reached, and the radiation density stays small even over a large part of the collapse phase of the cycle. The numerical increase in entropy of the whole model universe is almost entirely involved with the increasing rate at which the model expands and collapses, so there is plenty of opportunity within a cycle for the system to remain far from equilibrium in the thermodynamic sense for long periods. Bondi's profound observation concerning the blackness of the night sky and the brightness of the stars in it is entirely acceptable within the framework of the Landsberg-Park cosmology.

There is one very serious snag with the model as an alternative to the unique singularity of the Big Bang for an open universe. If successive cycles are larger and larger, and if the arrow of time is always the same, with entropy always increasing, we can see even without running the computer models backward that we still have a singular origin problem. Earlier cycles must have been both smaller and shorter lived, so that the bounce itself must have started in an infinitesimal hiccup some great number of cycles ago. The origin problem is still there, albeit in a slightly disguised form and rather longer ago. That does not mean that the Landsberg-Park model cannot tell us a lot about our own Universe. It does detract from its immediate appeal when we are deliberately seeking a possible description of the Universe which encompasses genuine rebirth, not a mere temporary imitation of rejuvenation that disguises an underlying continuing aging from a definite beginning to a rather less definite but nonetheless real ending many cycles ahead. As it happens, there is an even more attractive model, developed just before that of Landsberg and Park and based not on computer simulations but on the mathematics of relativity with, if you like, a touch of philosophy as well. The essential differences between the models arise from the treatment of the singularity at the beginning/end of the cycles, and, since this is the region we know least about, there is ample scope for a subjective choice in settling on the following description as the cosmology, if not of the Universe we do live in, then certainly of the universe I would like to be living in, and which, if there is any justice in the Universe, ought to be the real one.

The Means of Rejuvenation

If the Universe is truly to be reborn in the singularity which marks the beginning of one cycle and the end of another, and if the pattern of oscillations is to be the same many cycles ago as it is now and as it will be many cycles from now in the future, at some stage the system must be genuinely rejuvenated—somewhere the arrow of time must point in the opposite sense from the sense we are used to. As there seems no way in which the arrow of time can be redirected during any one cycle of expansion and collapse, the rejuvenation must be accomplished in a separate oscillatory cycle entirely. Just such a model has been put forward by Paul Davies, who also accomplished the feat of accounting for the origin of the cosmic background radiation within the framework of the same oscillatory model.

There is certainly no problem about defining the time at which the flow of entropy reverses in this model, since this is supposed to happen at the beginning/end singularity. The arrow of time is reversed in successive cycles so that our cycle follows a cycle of rejuvenation and will be succeeded by another similar cycle of rejuvenation, which in turn is followed by a cycle of increasing entropy just like the one in which we live, and so on. How can this account for the black-body background radiation? Quite simply, starlight that plunges into the hot, contracting fireball at the end of a cycle becomes scrambled, as indeed does the matter, until all correlations and information are lost. When the radiation re-emerges in the subsequent expansion, it must have the form of an isotropic background. Our cosmic background is the starlight from the previous cycle, and our starlight will be the background radiation in the next cycle—which neatly explains the otherwise puzzling coincidence that the energy density of the cosmic background radiation that fills our Universe is the same as the energy density of starlight spread across the Universe. It might seem that we still have an overall flow of the model universe from one cycle to the next, and the next, and so on, but Davies has a solution to that which restores symmetry in a startling yet beautifully simple way.

If the time-reversed cycle literally rejuvenates the universe into the state it was in at the beginning of the cycle, with the arrow of time we are used to, and if the forward cycle ages the model universe into exactly the same pre-rejuvenation state each time, then the distinction between successive *pairs* of cycles becomes not just confused but literally nonexistent. The model universe is closed in the spatial sense, because it re-collapses to a singularity; the model is also closed in a temporal sense, with the second half of a pair of cycles seen as closing the time loop and restoring the initial conditions. So, in Davies' model, not only space but space-time is closed, a much happier situation philosophically and more pleasing aesthetically. (See figure 6.) "We have," says Davies, "a picture of two temporal regions with oppositely directed time sense, separated by a small region in which there is no direction of time."

Had this remarkable model been put forward in the early sixties instead of in the early seventies, the discovery of the cosmic background might have been hailed as confirming its plausibility. Even with the background known before the theory was developed, there is food here for much thought about the nature of the Universe. Further studies by other cosmologists have only emphasized just how good a description of many puzzling features of the Universe the closed-time model is. D. T. Pegg of James Cook University, Australia, has examined the situation within the framework of the absorber theory of radiation and finds that with matter and antimatter in the two halves of the closed-time loop, the arrow of time must indeed be reversed in the way that Davies has

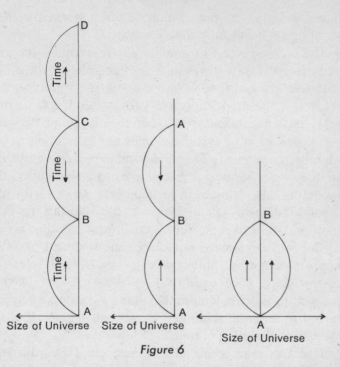

Figure 6

The Davies closed universe. In this model, each bounce is the same size with the arrow of time reversed in successive cycles to rejuvenate the universe. The model ages from A to B and then rejuvenates from B to C. The states A and C are therefore literally identical, as are states B and D and successive alternate states. This means the model can be shown simply as two cycles with opposite arrows of time and that the usual picture with time flowing constantly up the page can be restored by bending the two cycles so that the two indistinguishable states A are at the same place in the diagram. The universe now flows from A to B *with* the arrow of time and will flow from B back to A *against* the arrow of time. It makes no difference whether we measure size to the right or left of the line representing the flow of time.

suggested but not proved. M. G. Albrow of CERN, Geneva, has attempted to relate the microphysical properties of our Universe to those expected on Davies' model. Just as we have already seen that a positron moving forward in time is the exact equivalent of an electron moving backward in time, Albrow was able to show that the particles flowing forward in time, in the conventional sense, in our half of the closed space-time universe have their exact counterparts in the other half of the universe in the form of matter flowing backward in time, or antimatter flowing forward in time. "It is amusing to note," says Albrow, that the situation is "reminiscent of the well-known fluctuations of the vacuum in quantum electrodynamics, in which a virtual particle-antiparticle pair appears in free space and then annihilates."

We can thus restore symmetry and permanence to the Universe by building on the foundations laid by Davies' theorizing. Symmetry of space, symmetry of time, symmetry of matter, and even symmetry of radiation all fall neatly out of the theory. But the concept raises one important question—the eternal question of free will as opposed to determinism.

Avoiding the Cosmic Trap

If the Universe really does follow a symmetrical course in which there are literally only two cycles, with the end of one cycle being the beginning of the other and the end of the other being the beginning of the first, does this mean that we are doomed to an eternal and endless repetition of exactly the same scenes, like a looped movie film? Considering only the half of the loop in which time flows as we are used to it, must it follow that every repetition of the cycle, starting out from literally the very same white-hole explosion, must follow exactly the same course? We may have been here before, and, if we have, it might seem that we are predestined to follow the same beaten path that wc havc always trod. There is, I believe, a way out of this dilemma, if a dilemma it is. We may be saved from determinism by the uncertainty of events at the quantum level.

In the statistical sense—in thermodynamic terms—the Universe, if Davies is correct, goes from *A* to *B* to *C* only to discover that *C is A* and to begin again. Yet, remember that every time some physical system is confronted with a choice among possible quantum paths, it is believed to choose at random among the possible outcomes. We have already seen how this can be incorporated into the idea of multiply splitting parallel universes, with every possible outcome always occurring in some sense. Suppose there is only one Universe, that there are no parallels, but that the same Universe is repeatedly offered a choice between the same huge number of quantum paths. *There is no reason to expect it to choose the same quantum alternatives from those allowed every time the choice is offered.* Depending on just how different the outcomes of these quantum choices are, different cycles will still be different to a greater or lesser degree, just like the parallel universes envisaged by Piper. It's as if, instead of parallel universes running side by side, we have the parallel alternatives running one after another, with the more probable alternatives predominating. If it were not for the fact that all information is supposed to be scrambled in the singularity between cycles, it might be tempting to relate the situation to that strange feeling of déjà vu we all get from time to time—the feeling that something is almost, but not quite, repeating the pattern of an earlier sequence—or an earlier life. Perhaps there is a link between different parts of the cycle; perhaps we really are reborn as different people; perhaps there is a sound explanation of precognition and prophetic dreams. Perhaps—if only there were a way of communicating between halves of the universal cycle, or of storing information. Tachyons, again? Or could black-hole–white-hole tunnels burrow through space-time to upset the symmetry bit while in some way allowing information, as well as matter and radiation, to leak through? I've got this awful feeling that I really should know the answer to that one, if only I could put my finger on it. . . .

There are more things in Heaven and Earth, Horatio, than are dreamt of in your philosophy.

EPILOGUE:
Why Bother?

If only as entertainment, the story of white holes and the idea of the Universe itself as a repeating cosmic gusher deserves attention at a time when gloom and despondency abound in published world views. The argument that the kind of blue sky research that has given us this picture of the Universe is out of place in a world beset by the immediate problems produced by increasing population, dwindling resources, and limited food hardly holds up when we remember that the great imaginative leaps on which these ideas depend were all produced by the unaided power of human thought. On the contrary, it should be a source of considerable comfort in these troubled times that the human mind is still capable of such imaginative leaps and that we are far from the state of, say, the ant, whose food supply and practical engineering to provide accommodation dominate life to the exclusion of all else. A world in which there was no place for entertainment would be dull indeed, and a solution to the present problems that left room only for eating, working, and reproducing would be no solution at all.

Epilogue: Why Bother?

There should be no need for practical justification of man's inquisitiveness about the nature of the Universe and his place in it. To a human being, there is one overwhelming, compelling answer to the question, why bother to study the Universe?, and that is the classic, because it's there. The outward urge is part of human nature. If we did not wonder where we came from and where we are going, we would not be human.

This fundamental human inquisitiveness has been discussed by Jacob Bronowski in his fine book *The Ascent of Man*, wherein he comments, "Biologically, a human being is changeable, sensitive, mutable, fitted to many environments, and not static." Our inquisitiveness is part of the biology of being human. In philosophical terms, the justification for further research into the nature of the Universe has never been better expressed than by Bronowski's further words:

I am infinitely saddened to find myself suddenly surrounded in the West by a sense of terrible loss of nerve, a retreat from knowledge into—into what? Into Zen Buddhism; into falsely profound questions about, Are we not really just animals at bottom; into extrasensory perception and mystery. They do not lie along the line of what we are now able to know if we devote ourselves to it: an understanding of man himself. We are nature's unique experiment to make the rational intelligence prove itself sounder than the reflex. Knowledge is our destiny. Self-knowledge, at last bringing together the experience of the arts and the explanations of science, waits ahead of us.[1]

In more mundane, practical terms, there is still justification for this kind of research. One of the ways out of the present energy crisis, according to many people, lies in harnessing nuclear power effectively and safely, either by fission or by fusion. The theory on which our present ability to obtain nuclear power is built is, of course, Einstein's which he developed as pure research with no practical ends in mind. The energy that might be available from a hole in space is even more impressive, if only one could be found conveniently to hand, or manufactured. It is hard to see any practical application of this, but, in 1920, who foresaw any practical application of relativity theory? Certainly a better understanding of the fundamentals of gravity could be of great practical value—especially if some very recent experiments reported by Daniel Long of Eastern Washington State College are correct.

Long reports that the familiar inverse square law of gravity (force proportional to one over distance squared) may not hold for all distances. This is a sensational suggestion but no more sensational than the suggestion that time and space look different to observers moving relative to one another. Studies of planets and satellites show that the inverse square law works very precisely for distances greater than about 1,000 km, but it is extremely difficult to measure the gravitational force be-

246

tween two objects small enough to work with in the laboratory, since the constant of gravity is so small. There is also the problem of allowing for the influence of the earth's gravity on all the equipment in the laboratory. Now, such evidence as there is suggests a systematic shift in the nature of the gravitational constant with distances —the larger the separation, the larger the value of *G,* at least over short distances (in the experiments reported by Long, the distances were 4.5 cm and 30 cm).

This discovery is a happy one for speculators who can now allow *G* to vary with position (if only a little bit) as well as with time. And although the accepted value of *G* works well within the Solar System, even a very smal extra effect with increasing distance would yield values several percent bigger than the accepted value over large astronomical distances. This suggestion seems certain to be pounced upon by adherents of the oscillating universe model, as a slightly larger value of *G* at great distances will do very nicely to hold the Universe together and keep it bound. But the implications at the other extreme, at very small distances, are equally interesting.

If *G* decreases with distance, perhaps on the smallest scale of all, the attraction of gravity disappears—and it may even be replaced by a repulsive force not unlike some of the strange repulsive cores which a few astrophysicists have invoked to turn a collapsing massive body around into an expanding cosmic gusher. What the practical outcome of any such effect might be we cannot predict, any more than the Wright brothers could have predicted the development of the Concorde so soon after their first flight. The experiments may even be

wrong. But if we are ever to achieve an essentially un-
limited availability of energy, there seems little doubt
that it will come about through an improved understanding of the fundamental natural forces, including
gravity, and of the fundamental nature of space-time.
Our society needs technology, and new technology only
develops from new research; our society also needs
people who have a feeling for science and technology—
far more than are educated in science to any level today
—and how better to encourage interest in science than
by the realization that science is not dull but can be entertaining in its own right? Carl Sagan has summed the
situation up succinctly, referring especially to the United
States:

> Nuclear energy and rocket motors are the supreme
> examples of the choices technology sets for us: to
> harness the power of the sun for abundant energy
> —or to allow the destruction of our civilization
> in a nuclear holocaust; to carry nuclear destruction
> anywhere in the world—or to transport us to the
> planets and the stars. There is no turning back from
> technology. Of the 435 members of Congress, there
> are only two or three with professional training in
> science. There are no Senators with such back-
> grounds. In the Nixon administration there were
> no scientists with ready access to the highest level
> of government. The situation is sadly similar in
> other nations. The impoverished understanding of
> science at the top unfortunately but understandably
> reflects the situation in the public at large. This is
> madness.[2]

Sagan also agrees that science fiction can play a large part in introducing young people to science—it certainly did for both him and myself—but he, too, emphasizes that science fact is often even more entertaining than science fiction. In a comment which sums up my reasons for writing this book more eloquently than any phrases of mine:

> When I return to a science-fiction novel that I last read as a boy (and still remember with pleasure), it often seems to have deteriorated strangely over the years. What has really happened, I think, is my slow discovery that science is far more exciting than science fiction, far more intricate, far more subtle—and science has the additional virtue of being true.[3]

APPENDIX
Is Our Sun a Normal Star?

This Appendix was originally written for the Griffith Observer, *under the title "How 'Normal' is our Sun?" I include it here in its present form as a reminder that, although the broad sweep of the Universe and the mysteries of creation and our ultimate fate hold their inevitable fascination for the human imagination, there are equally fascinating puzzles to be found closer at hand. In many ways, the fact that we can ask the question, is our Sun a normal star? provides the supreme example of the unfettered vision which the human mind can achieve. Of course, it's common sense to think of our Sun as the archetypal star; a dog would no more wonder about the possibility of our star being an oddity among the many stars of the Milky Way than he would puzzle over why the sky is dark at night. The irreverence of the question, the way it sweeps aside common sense and dogma and, almost mischievously, asks the question, what if . . . ? provides a classic example of the kind of imagination that, on a rather larger scale, this book is all about.*

The Sun is the nearest star to us, dominating the Solar System and, it might naturally be thought, providing us

with the archetypal normal star against which astrophysicists can conveniently check their theories of stellar
structure. Until a decade or so ago, the Sun's track record
as an archetype was pretty good, and its mere existence
over the thousands of millions of years of the geological
record had been enough to show that the fusion of light
elements into heavier ones—nuclear burning—must be
the power source for the stars. Throughout the fifties, in
particular, the astrophysical implications of this nuclear
burning process were developed to the point where the
theory explained the existence of the variety of stars seen
in the Milky Way, including exotically named varieties
such as white dwarfs and red giants, while nova and
supernova explosions could be seen as the result of run-
away nuclear burning under critical conditions (although
it must be admitted that the details of supernovae, in particular, remain to be worked out satisfactorily even today).

In the late sixties and early seventies, however, astrophysicists have been faced with a series of puzzles, not
about the exotica of the Milky Way but about the Sun itself. There are two ways of looking at these puzzles; perhaps it's just that the Sun is so close that the warts show up
to spoil the beautiful agreement between theory and observation which seems to be there when we view stars
from further away. Or, perhaps, that agreement is genuine when we are dealing with stars in general, but no

longer holds true in detail when we are dealing with the special case of our own Sun. Either way, the situation is embarrassing; but before we can see how embarrassing it is, we need some idea of what the standard theories are.

Inside a star, the temperature reaches many millions of degrees, initially through the heat produced as the gravitational energy of a collapsing gas cloud is liberated. At these temperatures, atoms are completely stripped of their electrons so that the stellar material is a plasma—a sea of atomic nuclei (positively charged) mixed in with negatively charged electrons; as far as the nuclear fusion processes which maintain these temperatures after the initial collapse are concerned, we can ignore the electrons and briefly sketch in a somewhat oversimplified picture of the first steps on the nuclear fusion ladder.

Most of the nuclei are those of hydrogen—individual protons—which naturally tend to repel one another since they all carry the same positive electric charge. However, if the plasma is hot enough, then some of the protons have enough kinetic energy to overcome this repulsion during collisions and can combine in pairs. Each pair of protons that sticks together ejects one unit of positive charge (a positron, or anti-electron, which soon meets an electron in the plasma and is annihilated) leaving behind one proton and one neutron, a nucleus of deuterium (heavy hydrogen). Deuterium can then combine with another proton to produce helium-3 (two protons, one neutron) and two nuclei of helium-3 can get together to produce one nucleus of helium-4 (two protons, two neutrons) plus two ejected protons which go back into the pot. The net effect is that four protons have been converted into one nucleus of helium-4, and, along the way, a little mass (about 1 percent of the mass of four protons) has been converted into heat in line with Einstein's famous equation $E = mc^2$. The energy being produced by the Sun today is equivalent to the destruction of 4.5 million tonnes of mass every second, a mere fleabite compared with the total mass of the Sun, which is two-thousand-billion-billion tonnes (and English billions at that—each one a million million).

The nuclei of other elements are also built up in stars in chains of nuclear fusion reactions; more energy (which means a higher temperature) is needed for fusing more massive nuclei, and a star like the Sun is, according to theory, almost entirely powered by hydrogen burning. But a few unusually energetic nuclei are always around, and, even in the Sun, occasional reactions build up elements more complex than helium—and occasional soon mounts up, by terrestrial standards, when such a large mass of material is involved. This is why that picture is an oversimplification.

Still, it seems worth sketching the later stages of evolution of a star in an equally simple way. As hydrogen burning continues, the center of the star eventually becomes clogged with an ash of helium nuclei, so that eventually the heat generated is no longer sufficient to hold the star up against gravity. When that point arrives, the core of the star collapses and heats up, and, with more energy to play with, helium nuclei start to fuse together in large numbers. In this helium burning stage, the extra heat from the compact core forces the outer layers of the star to expand, and it becomes a giant; meanwhile, the fusing of more massive nuclei begins to build up more interesting (as far as we are concerned) elements, including carbon and oxygen. These elements are dispersed across the Galaxy when stars explode at the end of the stage of stable nuclear burning; they eventually find a place in the clouds of interstellar material, from which new stellar and planetary systems form, planets on which living creatures composed chiefly of heavy elements (like ourselves) can evolve.

The real evidence that all these nuclear processes go on inside stars came with the success of computer models in which numerical simulations of the various nuclear processes, together with specification of the mass of a star, are sufficient to produce a numerical model predicting that a star of a certain mass and age will have a certain temperature (or color) and composition. Such models predict that a star of one solar mass and the same age as our Sun will be as bright as the Sun and have the size of our Sun—or very nearly. It is the gap between exactly and very nearly that leads us to question the normality of our Sun.

The Neutrino Puzzle

Ten years ago, it seemed that only the details of stellar nucleosynthesis remained to be worked out and that we understood the workings of an ordinary star like the Sun pretty thoroughly. This view was wrong, and it was shown to be wrong when it became possible, according to the best theories, to make direct observations of something happening in the interior of the Sun. But that something turns out not to be there—and that discovery (or lack of discovery) is what upset the theorists' applecart.

Conventional observations of the Sun and stars depend on monitoring the electromagnetic radiation from their surfaces, but a photon struggling out from the interior can take millions of years to reach the surface, being involved in many collisions and interactions on the way. Conventional astronomy tells us only about the average conditions inside the star—an average effectively taken over this very long time-scale for radiation to travel through the hot plasma. To the great pioneers of the theory of stellar structure, such as Eddington, the concept of a particle than can travel from the center of the Sun out and across space to reach the Earth in only a few minutes would have seemed almost magical, but those pioneers would certainly have appreciated the value of such a particle to anyone wishing to study the reactions going on in the solar interior today. Just such a particle, the neutrino, is now an essential feature of our best theories of nuclear physics, and evidence for the existence of neutrinos has come from many experiments involving particle interactions here on Earth. According to these theories, many nuclear reactions cannot work without neutrinos being involved; indeed, it's just because certain reactions do occur that neutrinos are believed to exist. But the neutrino is an odd bird. It has no mass, it travels at the speed of light, and carries spin. It is so unsociable that only one neutrino in every hundred-thousand million produced in the Sun should, according to theory, fail to escape into space. To a neutrino, the fiery Sun and solid Earth are scarcely more of an obstruction than empty space itself. Yet elusive though they may be, according to those same best theories, 3 percent of the energy radiated by the Sun is in the form of neutrinos, and about one-hundred-thousand-million solar neutrinos cross every square centimeter of the Earth (including you, me, and this page) every second. That is so many that we ought to be able to catch some with suitable detectors, even though they are reluctant to interact with anything at all. It would be hopeless to try to catch one solitary neutrino, but reasonable enough to hope to trap a few out of that hundred-thousand million crossing each square centimeter each second.

In the attempt to do that, researchers have built detectors as large as a swimming pool, buried deep in a mine underground where the influence of everything except neutrinos is screened out by layers of rock, filled with carbon tetrachloride, because neutrinos are believed to be partial to some of the nuclei of the chlorine in that compound. In theory, a few solar neutrinos should interact with the isotope chlorine-37, with the end result that a few atoms of argon-37 will be produced in the tank of fluid, and argon-37 is much easier to detect than a neutrino. The snag is that the solar neutrinos simply refuse to appear; no argon-37 attributable to solar neutrino interactions is being found in the tanks.

If any solar neutrinos have been detected, it is only in the very latest series of observations reported by Ray Davis and his colleagues, who run the experiment at the Homestake Goldmine in South Dakota. Over a decade, the experiments came up with negative results, but, in the last year or so, a few argon-37 nuclei that *might* have been produced by solar neutrino interactions have been found in the tank. This could be a coincidence, or it could mean that the Sun has lately started emitting the neutrinos that should, in theory, have been there all along. That is something astronomers are still arguing about, but, either way, one thing is clear. Over most of the past ten years, the Sun has certainly not been producing the steady flux of neutrinos expected on the

Appendix

basis of our best theories of stellar structure and of nuclear physics. Only two possibilities are allowed, assuming the observations are correct. Either the theories of nuclear physics are wrong, or the theories of stellar structure are wrong when applied to the Sun.

Now, the particle interactions can be tested to some extent using accelerators on Earth; the results of those experiments provide the basis of the theory suggesting that the Sun should produce a lot of neutrinos. It is very difficult to see how the nuclear and particle physics theories could be adjusted slightly to explain away the lack of solar neutrinos in Davis' tank. Several theorists have tried more or less bizarre adjustments to the theory, but none of them really work; on the other hand, it is very easy to adjust the structure of a computer model of a one-solar-mass star to switch off the flow of neutrinos. All you need to do is turn down the temperature of the nuclear cooker slightly—by about 10 percent—which is enough to turn off the nuclear reactions which are expected to produce most of the neutrinos. Of course, that can only be a temporary solution, since the Sun needs those reactions to keep it hot.

But is it possible that the Sun has actually gone temporarily off the boil? Remember, if this idea is correct, the lack of neutrinos indicates that the Sun's interior is a little cooler right now than on average; the surface brightness, on the other hand, merely confirms the temperature of the interior averaged over many millions of years. If the nuclear fusion in the interior were switched off entirely, the Sun would not go out like a light but would settle down slowly over about 30 million years. The geological and other records show that the Sun has been burning fairly steadily, thanks to nuclear fusion, for thousands of millions of years; but the inbuilt safety valve provided by its store of gravitational potential energy means that it can continue superficially unchanged for several millions of years if something does happen to disturb the normal nuclear burning. So, on the face of things, the neutrino evidence suggests that the Sun is not in a normal state just now. Not normal, that is, when compared either to its own long history or to the present state of most stars in the Milky Way. The problem then becomes one of explaining how and why the Sun might have gone off the boil temporarily—and it turns out that a plausible possibility has been around for more than twenty-five years, associated with a theory of ice ages. As an explanation of ice ages, the theory isn't all that convincing, but Öpik's ideas about intermittent convective mixing in the Sun seem appropriate in the context of the modern solar neutrino problem.

Ice Ages and the Sun

The basis for the model is that, from time to time, conditions inside the Sun may become appropriate for convective mixing to occur over a large part of the interior, producing first an increase in heat and associated expansion of the outer layers (slightly) as more hydrogen fuel is mixed into the nuclear burning region, then a phase of cooling and contraction as conditions return toward the long-term equilibrium. The idea has recently been picked up by several theorists, including Willy Fowler, and even linked with theories of climatic change on Mars. The difficulty with all these ideas is that no one has explained why the convective mixing should happen to have occurred in the recent past. The problem is still there, but one step further removed; no solar neutrinos because of recent mixing—but why recent mixing?

Late in 1975, a possible answer appeared in another theory of ice ages, curiously with no mention of the implications for solar neutrinos. Bill McCrea presented his model of how the interaction of the Sun with the dark lanes of compressed material which define the spiral arms of our Galaxy could produce ice ages, comets, and, originally, the Solar System itself. That is quite a story. (*Observatory* magazine, December 1975). The important point is that the Sun can be affected by the dust it gathers while crossing through such a spiral and that we have just passed through the dust lane associated with the Orion arm—indeed, we may even have passed through the dense material of the Orion nebula itself—emerging less than twenty thousand years ago. If the dust accreting onto the Sun can trigger the convective instability, we are home and dry; a disturbance only twenty thousand years old would certainly not yet have been worked through the Sun's system and equilibrium restored. But how can we test the idea?

Once again, we come back to the computer models. The Sun gathering material from a cloud of dust is somewhat like a star in a binary system gathering material from its neighbor, and many people have run computer simulations of that situation. What they show is that the energy from the infalling material causes alterations in the outer layers of the star with a very slight decrease in the rate of nuclear burning and a tendency to stabilize the star against convective instability. That seems just the opposite of the effect we are looking for; but what happens when the extra material stops falling in, when the Sun emerges from the cloud of dust? This is hard to answer; the computer models have not been able to produce meaningful answers when asked that question. In computer jargon, the models fail to converge. That in itself could be taken as indicating the possibility of instabilities setting in—computer models find it hard to cope with sudden changes. And in physical terms, if adding material inhibits convection, suddenly ceasing to add material could certainly encourage the spread of convection, in a way similar to the effects of removing the lid from a pressure cooker. Such evidence as there is, and admittedly it is not conclusive, suggests that *emergence* from a dust cloud could indeed trigger convective instability, allowing the temperature of the solar interior to drop temporarily by the 10 percent or so needed to stop the production of large quantities of neutrinos. To some extent the evidence is circumstantial, but since McCrea's ideas were published, other circumstantial evidence pointing the same way has also appeared.

One piece of this evidence is the detection of oscillations in the Sun, which have been likened to earthquakes and which astrophysicists hope to use to develop an understanding of the solar interior in a manner akin to the way seismology reveals details of the Earth's interior structure. One fly in the ointment, discussed at the Royal Astronomical Society's March 1976 meeting, is that one of the first oscillations detected, with a period of two hours and forty minutes, can be conveniently explained in terms of a stellar model with an interior 10 percent cooler than the standard solar models. This is not, at the time of writing, the most widely favored explanation of this discovery, but it seems a remarkable coincidence that this temperature is in line with the temperature needed to account for the absence of neutrinos today.

The other clue comes from climatic studies. Researchers at the National Center for Atmospheric Research in Boulder, Colorado, have looked again at the old idea that sunspots are associated with changes in the weather and that climate varies in line with the changing level of solar activity. By including a variation of the amount of heat radiated by the Sun (the solar constant, which they now dub the solar parameter), these researchers can explain many features of changing global temperatures over the past three centuries. The variation they allow seems remarkable to an astronomer brought up to think of the Sun as a steady, stable star—as much as 2 percent over the eleven-year cycle. Most remarkable of all, however, is that such observations of the solar parameter do not rule out the reality of such a variation.

Recent observations of the outer planets show that their brightnesses vary over the roughly eleven-year sunspot cycle by just this amount (2 percent), although, again, no one seems to believe this is an effect of the changing solar parameter, but that it is due to changes in the composition of the clouds in the atmospheres of those planets, brought about by photochemical effects linked with the changing solar cycle. Another coincidence? The crucial point is that we simply do not know if the Sun varies by 1 or 2 percent over eleven years or so, and we will not know until the next generation of satellites makes the necessary observations from above the confusing layers of the Earth's atmosphere. Meanwhile, we must turn to the evidence available from observations of stars in general, which can be compared to each other to eliminate changes caused by changes in the transparency of the air. These show unambiguously that normal stars like the Sun do not vary by 2 percent within periods of eleven years or so. Clearly, either the NCAR theory of recent climatic changes is wrong or the Sun is not a normal star. In the light of the solar neutrino evidence, which alternative looks more plausible?

The overall situation is tantalizing. We certainly have enough evidence of one kind and another to make the question, how normal is our Sun?, one worth asking, but we do not at present have enough information for an unequivocal answer. This is a vital question for physicists pushing our understanding of the laws of physics to the limit, since if the Sun is *not* normal, then their theories are on surer ground; equally, as the link with ideas of climatic change (whether it be ice ages or the smaller fluctuations of the past three centuries) shows, this question is of widespread interest. We may not all be concerned about details of the laws of physics, but we are certainly all concerned about changes in the Sun which can affect the climate on Earth. It is also useful to ponder the evidence that the development of man as an intelligent, adaptable creature was influenced in no small measure by the advance and retreat of the ice tens of thousands of years ago; we may owe our very existence on Earth to the same astronomical factors responsible for the abnormal state of the Sun today. As McCrea has commented, "Life can be very complicated."

GLOSSARY

Antimatter

Ordinary matter has a counterpart at a fundamental (sub-atomic) level in a mirror-image kind of matter with opposite properties. For example, an electron has a negative charge and its antimatter equivalent, the positron, carries the same size positive charge. Because mass and energy are interchangeable, pairs of particles, one matter and the other antimatter, can be crested spontaneously from intense radiation fields. Conversely, whenever a particle meets its antimatter counterpart, the two are destroyed in an intense burst of energy.

Black hole

Any object with such a strong gravitational pull that not even light can escape from it is called a black hole.

Cepheid variable

Many stars vary in brightness. The Cepheids are unusual because the length of variation of their periodic cycle of brightness depends on the average brightness (over the whole cycle) of each star. So, by measuring the period of a Cepheid astronomers can deduce how bright it is; then, by measuring how bright it seems from Earth they can tell how far away the star is, just as a measure of the apparent brightness of a 100-watt bulb would indicate the distance to it. Cepheids are the standard candles which establish the baseline for all astronomical distance estimates beyond our immediate neighborhood.

Compression lane

Gas clouds moving between the stars in galaxies often collide and produce hot, compressed regions of material. Permanent compression lanes mark the edges of the spiral arms characteristic of many galaxies; these are probably produced by standing shock waves—a spiral blast pattern on a galactic scale.

Dwarf star

As a small star ages and its nuclear fuel is exhausted, it collapses into a so-called dwarf and gradually cools, passing through a white, a red, and, ultimately, a black stage. A black dwarf is not a black hole, however, but an old, cold star which is black because no more radiation is being produced from it.

Electromagnetic radiation

Visible light, X-rays, infrared heat, and radio are all forms of electromagnetic radiation, produced by the interaction of charged particles (chiefly electrons) with magnetic fields.

Electron

One of the fundamental building blocks of atoms. All atoms are composed of protons and neutrons bound in a compact nucleus, surrounded by clouds of electrons. The mass of one electron is about 9×10^{-28} gm, that is, 0.(27 zeros)9 gm.

Energy

Everything is energy, and the Universe is a device which converts one form of energy into another. Water flowing downhill converts gravitational energy into energy of motion; a rocket struggling upward converts the heat energy of its fuel into gravitational and kinetic energy; even solid matter can be completely converted to energy (if, perhaps, it meets up with antimatter) in line with Einstein's equation $E = mc^2$.

Escape velocity

In order to escape from the gravitational pull of any object, the escaping object must have enough kinetic energy. A ball thrown upward will go higher if it is thrown harder; at a certain speed, it would go so high that it would never fall back—the minimum speed for this to happen is called the escape velocity. The kinetic energy given by the escape velocity is enough to balance the gravitational energy of attraction between the home planet (or star) and the escaping object.

Event horizon

As an object falls into a black hole, a point is reached at which the escape velocity exceeds the speed of light. This is the event horizon, so called since no events which occur inside it can ever be observed from outside, since no light can escape to reach the would-be observers.

Fission/fusion

When some heavy elements are divided or fissioned at the atomic level, they produce daughter products in which the mass of the new atoms produced from each old atom is, in total, a little less than the mass of the atom that split. The extra mass has been converted into electromagnetic radiation—the basis of fission reactors and atomic bombs. Conversely, some very light atoms (of elements such as helium) can, under the right conditions, combine to produce more massive atoms, in a process resulting in a new atom containing less mass than the sum of the masses of the combining atoms. Once again, the excess mass is converted to energy in the form of electromagnetic radiation. Fusion (hydrogen) bombs operate in this way, but fusion is most important as the power source of the stars.

Fission and fusion both operate because it is the middle range of elements (by mass) which are most stable. If undisturbed, all matter would naturally incline toward fission or fusion processes leading to the conversion of all matter into iron. Dwarf stars probably represent such an end-point of nuclear fusion—hot lumps of iron, as massive as our Sun, slowly cooling in space.

Gravity

No one knows what gravity is, although we can describe it. Any two objects with masses m and $n,$ say, will be attracted to each other with a force Gmn/r^2, where G is the constant of gravity and r the separation of the two objects. This force binds stars and galaxies, drives atoms close enough together for fusion to operate in stars, and can distort the very fabric of space, opening gates to other times and other places. But we can no more say what gravity *is* than we can explain color to a blind person.

Hubble's constant

Observations of distant galaxies suggest that they (and we) are involved in a universal expansion, in which the relative speed of separation of a pair of galaxies is proportional to their separation. The constant of proportionality is named after the discoverer of this relation, Hubble.

Mach's principle

The idea that everything in the Universe is influenced by everything else, in particular the idea that an object possesses inertia (reluctance to begin to move or to be pushed into a new path) because the Universe as a whole in some way strives to maintain the status quo.

Magnetism

Like gravity, magnetism is basically a mystery. It is the force produced by charged particles moving in flowing electric currents, and can be locked up in such devices as bar magnets, presumably because they contain tiny cells of flowing current. Unlike gravity, magnetism comes in two varieties, and pairs of North and South poles are, as far as we know, always associated with one another. Like poles repel, opposites attract, and both influence charged particles such as electrons.

Mass

Energy can be locked up in compact packets which can themselves have such properties as magnetic or electric activity. At the most fundamental level these packets are best described in terms of wave vibration, but when enough packets join together they take on the properties of what we know as solid particles and join in further hierarchies to make complex solid objects which are in reality chiefly empty space with a leavening of wave packets. The mass of an object is a measure of how much energy is locked up in it in this form, and indicates how strong the gravity of the object is.

N-galaxy

A galaxy with an energetically active nucleus.

Neutrino

An elusive particle which is produced in some reactions involving elementary particles (such as fusion) but, once produced, is reluctant to react with any other particle. Because of this, one astronomer was heard to remark that the Universe must be swimming in a sea of clapped out neutrinos. Our Sun, however, doesn't seem to be producing the expected flood of neutrinos from the fusion processes which keep it hot, and this has led to speculation that our Sun may not be a normal star.

Neutron

One of the three basic particles (or packets of energy) from which atoms are built up.

Olbers' paradox

In an infinitely large universe full of stars, in any direction we look we would see a star, and the sky would be a permanent blaze of light. So the dark night sky tells us that the Universe is either finite, or not full of stars, or both—or that the light energy in the Universe is being dissipated by the red shift associated with a universal expansion.

Parsec

A measure of distance used in astronomy. In one year, light can travel about 9.5 billion (million million) km at a speed of some 1.1 thousand million km per hour —this is the measure of distance termed a light-year. A parsec is the distance at which the Earth's orbit would subtend an angle of one second of arc, about 3.26 light-years.

Photon

The packet of energy associated with a fundamental unit of electromagnetic energy.

Planck's constant

The energy E of a photon with frequency v is given by $E = hv$, where h is Planck's constant. The constant also appears in other fundamental relations of this kind.

Plasma

Material which is so hot that electrons have been stripped from individual atoms to produce a sea of negatively charged electrons in which the positively charged nuclei swim.

Positron

An antielectron (see antimatter).

Proton

The third of the building blocks from which atoms are made, the proton carries a positive charge equal in magnitude to the electron's negative charge, but its mass is almost the same as that of a neutron, about 1,000 times the mass of an electron.

Pulsar

A compact star produced as the leftover ember of a stellar explosion, spinning very rapidly and producing, through its magnetism and charged particles, very regular bursts of radio noise.

Quark

The so-called fundamental particles (such as electrons, protons, and neutrons) are believed to be built up from yet more fundamental packets of energy known as quarks. Since no one has found a quark and kept it for study, theorists have not yet been encouraged to ponder what quarks are made of. One theory, however, holds that the universe may have started out as a quark soup.

Quasar

Any object which appears on a simple photographic plate to be an ordinary star, but which shows a red shift indicating great distance (beyond the fringes of our Galaxy) is named a quasar, short for quasistellar object.

Red shift

If a moving car sounds a horn, the note will seem higher if the car moves toward you and lower if it

moves away. This Doppler effect also happens with
light, but is only noticeable at high speeds because the
speed of light itself so great. A shift of light toward
the red end of the spectrum, or red shift, indicates that
a distant galaxy or quasar is moving rapidly away from
us.

Relativity

The theory of the Universe developed first by Einstein
in which many properties of objects are seen to be not
absolute but relative to their relation to other objects.
A moving rod, for instance, is shorter than its stationary
counterpart, and time runs more slowly for a moving
clock.

Schwarzschild radius

When a star (or other mass) is squeezed within a
critical radius, gravity takes over and turns it into a
black hole. The critical radius is named after the
mathematician Schwarzschild who formulated the relevant equations.

Seyfert galaxy

An explosively active galaxy, probably part of the same
family of white-hole gushers as quasars and N-galaxies.

Singularity

In a massive black hole, matter can be crushed ir-
resistibly by gravity until all the mass is contained in a
mathematical point, or singularity. Generally, such a
singularity will be hidden behind an event horizon, but
in certain rotating objects a naked singularity, which
can interact with the rest of the Universe, might form.
Such naked singularities might provide entrances to
tunnels through the fabric of space-time.

Supernova

The nuclear fusion reactions in some large stars can
run away to produce a vast explosion in which the

energy liberated from one star is temporarily as much as is usually produced in a whole galaxy of, for example, a thousand million stars like our Sun. Such explosions leave behind very compact stellar cinders, often seen as pulsars.

Tachyon

A hypothetical particle which travels faster than the speed of light. If tachyons exist, they inhabit a curious Alice-in-Wonderland world where they can only slow down by *gaining* energy; they might also be thought of as traveling backward in time in some circumstances.

White hole

Just as matter can collapse into a black-hole singularity, so a singularity might pour matter outward into our Universe in the cosmic gusher of a white hole.

X-ray

Very energetic (high frequency) electromagnetic radiation.

NOTES

INTRODUCTION

[1] And those less recent—some of the most obvious lessons from free-fall conditions demonstrate the accuracy not of Einstein's imagination, but of Newton's.

PROLOGUE 2

[1] Except in rare cases where a neutron star near the mass limit might accrete a little extra material by the tug of its gravity acting on the tenuous gas of interstellar space.

[2] Stars that emit precisely timed pulses of radio noises that are explained as being from a beam of radiation sweeping around from a spinning neutron star, like the beam of a lighthouse.

[3] The descriptive terminology for this points out the poetry in the souls of astronomers. We have already encountered stars known as degenerate white dwarfs; in terms of the standard diagram on which astronomers trace the evolution of stars, the giant with a helium burning core becomes "a red giant sitting on the horizontal branch." It then seems, of course, only natural that in due course the giant should

fall from its precarious perch, which indeed it does, eventually becoming a white dwarf in the process.

4 Even the science fictioneers had an imagination failure in this regard. In his otherwise excellent story "Neutron Star," published in 1968, just about as the discovery of pulsars was announced, Larry Niven described an encounter with an object known as BVS-1, described as being the only known neutron star. In a novel published in 1973, which described future events occurring before those of "Neutron Star" (science-fiction authors have their own ways of traveling in time), the same writer described another encounter with the same object, but now described as the "first *nonrotating* [my italics] neutron star ever discovered. Atypical compared with pulsars . . . difficult to find." The hero is required to comment in justification of his apparently suicidally close approach to the star: "I wouldn't dare dive into the radiating gas shell around a pulsar, but this beast seems to have a long rotation period and no gas envelope at all . . . it must be an old one." [It's a pity that the rest of that particular novel (surely Niven's least satisfactory to date) is not as well thought out as that explanation.]

CHAPTER ONE

1 *Cosmology Now,* ed. Laurie John.
2 Ibid.
3 *Cosmology Now.*
4 This is why the light-year is used as a measure of astronomical distance, not of time; it is the distance light can travel in space in one year.
5 *Cosmology Now.*
6 "Was There Really a Big Bang?"

CHAPTER TWO

[1] Free charged particles (such as protons and electrons) could interact with radiation to some extent—producing bursts of photons if the charged particles were accelerated by a magnetic field, for example.
[2] "It's Done with Mirrors."
[3] *Mercury.*

CHAPTER THREE

[1] *Modern Astronomy.*
[2] *Mercury.*
[3] "The Arrow of Time."

CHAPTER FOUR

[1] In common with other authors of science fiction over the past four decades, Niven gets around this little difficulty by invoking hyperspace, a region cut off from the Universe in which the ordinary laws of physics do not apply and the speed of spacecraft is not limited to the speed of light. In such a region, a spaceship that can move in and out of hyperspace at will can achieve instant space travel. Of course, there are a few snags for the practical minded. Hyperspace may exist and black and white holes may provide entrances and exits to hyperspace, although only a madman would try to find out by flying a spacecraft into a black hole. The big snag is that to tunnel a way into or out of hyperspace would require a lot of energy—more than the total gravitational energy of our Sun; otherwise, the Sun it-

self would pop off into hyperspace through a black hole. That is a little too much energy for the motors of any practicable spaceship.

Still, a good yarn remains a good yarn, and it is the deviations from proved science that make science-fiction stories *fiction*. I've no objection to Niven's tales of the explosion of the galactic core on those grounds, but he might have done his homework a little better before trying to describe the nature of the explosion. The idea of stars packed so closely together that a chain reaction of supernova explosions can spread across the core, each exploding star triggering at least two more into instability, sounds dramatic enough, but he'll never make a quasar that way. Laplace could have pointed out to him that a multitude of stars packed that closely together would cause a large black hole from which no light or radiation could escape, so that if the supernovas did explode inside the hole there would be nothing to worry about. The author of "Neutron Star" should have enough knowledge of gravity to appreciate that. Quasars and exploding galactic nuclei (which are probably the same thing) are an order of incomprehensibility bigger and better than any collection of supernovae.
2 See Appendix.
3 *The Milky Way*.
4 Ibid.

CHAPTER FIVE

1 White Holes and High Energy Astrophysics.
2 *Foundation*.
3 *The Next Ten Thousand Years*.
4 In *Cosmology Now*.
5 *Black Holes*.

6 *BBC Science Magazine.*

7 Ibid.

8 *Maker of Universes, A Private Cosmos, The Gates of Creation.*

CHAPTER SIX

1 *Cosmology Now.*

2 Ibid.

3 The best known of these, perhaps, are the "spindizzies" that power James Blish's *Cities in Flight;* we are told that the theory behind these impressive devices rests upon the foundation of the Blackett-Dirac equations, which "show a relationship between magnetism and the spinning of a massive body—that much is the Dirac part of it . . . both magnetism *and* gravity are phenomena of rotation." Echos here of Mach's principle again! Dirac's name has also been used in connection with the "Dirac pusher drive" which is mentioned in passing in several tales involving travel to the stars. But, alas, there is no real physical basis for these drives—the introduction of Dirac's name and a couple of equations is just window dressing. Still, Dirac himself has done more than enough to justify his own place in the story of how local events are influenced by the Universe at large.

4 *Modern Cosmology.*

5 "Dirac Completes His Theory of Large Numbers."

6 Dirac is far from alone in playing the numbers game. It has also involved such eminent astronomers as Eddington and, in recent years, a clutch of Soviet workers whose ideas have been reveiewed by Paul Davies in an article, "Russian Cosmology," in *Nature.*

7 "On the Nature of Mass."

8 Edited by Kenneth Brecher and Giancarlo Setti.

CHAPTER SEVEN

[1] *Ring Around the Sun.*
[2] *Analog.*
[3] "How Special Is the Universe?"
[4] "Is the Universe a Vacuum Fluctuation?"
[5] Ibid.
[0] "Antimatter."
[7] *Gravity and Neutrinos: Paradoxes and Possibilities.*

EPILOGUE

[1] *The Ascent of Man.*
[2] *The Cosmic Connection.*
[3] Ibid.

BIBLIOGRAPHY

Aharony, A., and Y. Ne'eman. "Time-Reversal Symmetry Violation and the Oscillating Universe." *International Journal of Theoretical Physics* **3** (1970):437.

Albrow, M. G. "CPT Conservation in the Oscillating Model of the Universe." *Nature Physical Science* **241** (1971):56.

Ambartsumian, V. A. In *Report on 11th Solvay Conference.* 1958.

————. In *Report on 13th Solvay Conference.* 1964.

Anderson, Poul. *Tau Zero.* London: Gollancz, 1970.

Anonymous. "The Universe Considered as a Hole." *Nature* **232** (1971):56.

————. "Invoking Black Holes." *Nature* **243** (1973):114.

Arp, H. *Atlas of Peculiar Galaxies.* Pasadena: CalTech, 1966.

————. "The Quasar Controversy." Interview in *Mercury* **3** (1974):6.

Asimov, Isaac. *Foundation.* New York: Doubleday, 1951.

————. *The Stars Like Dust.* New York: Doubleday, 1953.

————. *The Gods Themselves.* London: Gollancz, 1972.

————. "The Endochronic Properties of Resublimated Thiotimoline." First published in *Astounding Science Fiction,* March 1948; reprinted in *The Early Asimov,* vol. 3. London: Panther, 1974.

Bibliography

Bahcall, John, and Jeremiah Ostriker. "Massive Black Holes in Globular Clusters?" *Nature* **256** (1975):23.

Bardeen, J. M., B. Carter, and S. W. Hawking. "The Four Laws of Black Hole Mechanics." *Communications in Mathematical Physics* **31** (1973):161.

Berry, Adrian. *The Next Ten Thousand Years.* London: Jonathan Cape, 1974.

Blish, James. *Cities in Flight.* New York: Avon Books, 1970.

Bok, B. J., and P. F. Bok. *The Milky Way.* 4th ed. Cambridge, Mass.: Harvard University Press, 1974

Bondi, H. "Setting the Scene," in: *Cosmology Now,* ed. by Laurie John. London: BBC Publications, 1973.

Brecher, K., and G. Setti, eds. *High Energy Astrophysics and Its Relation to Elementary Particle Physics.* Cambridge, Mass.: MIT Press, 1974. See especially, K. H. Prendergast, "Structure and Dynamics of Galaxies," p. 415, and John Wheeler's discussion of singularities, p. 519.

Bronowski, J. *The Ascent of Man.* London: BBC Publications, 1973.

Bruce, C. E. R. "The Role of Lightning in Astrophysical Phenomena." *Observatory* **95** (1975):204.

Burbidge, G. "Was There Really a Big Bang?" *Nature* **253** (1971):36.

————, and M. Burbidge. Interview in *Mercury* **4** (1975): 11.

————, and Fred Hoyle. "Antimatter." *Scientific American Offprint.* No. 202. San Francisco: W. H. Freeman, 1958.

Calder, Nigel. *Violent Universe.* London: BBC Publications, 1969.

Carr, B. J. "The Primordial Black Hole Mass Spectrum." *Orange Aid Preprint,* OAP-389. Pasadena: CalTech, 1975.

————, and S. W. Hawking. "Black Holes in the Early

Universe." *Monthly Notices of the Royal Astronomical Society* **168** (1974):399.

Carroll, Lewis. *The Annotated Alice*. Ed. by Martin Gardner. London: Penguin, 1965.

————. *The Annotated Snark*. London: Penguin, 1967.

Cavallo, G. "Interpretation of the Dirac Relationship Between Fundamental Constants." *Nature* **245** (1973):313.

Clay, Roger, and Philip Crouch. "Possible Observations of Tachyons Associated With Extensive Air Showers." *Nature* **248** (1974):28.

Collins, C. B., and S. W. Hawking. "The Rotation and Distortion of the Universe." *Monthly Notices of the Royal Astronomical Society* **162** (1973):307.

————, and M. J. Perry. "Superdense Matter: Neutrons or Asymptotically Free Quarks?" *Physical Review Letters* **34** (1975):1353.

Craine, E. R., S. Tapia, and M. Tarenghi. "New Non-stellar BL-Lacertae Objects." *Nature* **258** (1975):56.

Crew, E. W. "Lightning in Astronomy." *Nature* **252** (1974):539.

Dahlbacka, G. H., G. F. Chapline, and T. A. Weaver. "Gamma Rays from Black Holes." *Nature* **250** (1974):36.

Das, P. K. "Gravitational Redshifts and Angular Diameters of Collapsed Objects." *Monthly Notices of the Royal Astronomical Society* **172** (1975):673.

————, and J. V. Narlikar. "Central Gravitational Redshifts from Static Massive Objects." *Monthly Notices of the Royal Astronomical Society* **171** (1975):87.

Davies, P. C. W. "Closed Time as an Explanation of the Black Body Background Radiation." *Nature Physical Science* **240** (1972):3.

————. "How Special Is the Universe?" *Nature* **249** (1974):208.

————. "Russian Cosmology." *Nature* **250** (1974):373.

Bibliography

————. "Dirac Completes His Theory of Large Numbers." *Nature* **250** (1974):460.

————. *The Physics of Time Asymmetry.* University of California Press, 1974.

————. "Astrophysics and Energy from Black Holes." *Nature* **251** (1974):12.

————. "A New Theory of the Universe." *Nature* **253** (1975):191.

————. "Opening Up the Universe." *Nature* **253** (1975): 594.

————, and J. G. Taylor. "Do Black Holes Really Explode?" *Nature* **250** (1974):37.

Davis, Talmadge, and John Ray. *Gravity and Neutrinos: Paradoxes and Possibilities.* Essay awarded Honorable Mention by the Gravity Research Foundation of New Boston, 1975.

Dawson, W. F., and Ben Bova. "It's Done with Mirrors." *Analog,* **LXXIV**, April 1965, p. 9.

Demiánski, M., and J. P. Lasota. "Black Holes in an Expanding Universe." *Nature Physical Science* **241** (1973): 53.

Dirac, P.A.M. "The Cosmological Constants." *Nature* **139** (1937):323.

————. "Long Range Forces and Broken Symmetries." *Proceedings of the Royal Society* **A333** (1973):408.

————. "Cosmological Models and the Large Numbers Hypothesis." *Proceedings of the Royal Society* **A338** (1974):439.

Eardley, D. M. "Death of White Holes in the Early Universe." *Physical Review Letters* **33** (1974):442.

Farmer, Philip José. *Maker of Universes.* London: Sphere, 1970.

————. *A Private Cosmos.* London: Sphere, 1970.

————. *The Gates of Creation.* London: Sphere, 1970.

Faulkner, John. "*G*-Wizardry at Dallas." *Nature* **253** (1975):231.

Field, G. B., H. Arp, and J. N. Bahcall. *The Redshift Controversy*. New York: Benjamin, 1973.

Frederick, L. W., and R. H. Baker. *An Introduction to Astronomy*. 8th ed. New York: Van Nostrand, 1974.

Fuller, R. W., and J. A. Wheeler. "Causality and Multiply-Connected Space-Time." *Physical Review* **128** (1962): 919.

Gamow, George. "The Evolutionary Universe." *Scientific American Offprint* No. 211. San Francisco: W. H. Freeman, 1956.

Gibbons, G. W. "On Lowering a Rope into a Black Hole." *Nature Physical Science* **240** (1972):77.

Gibbons, Garry. "Black Holes are Hot." *New Scientist* **69** (1976):54.

Goldhaber, M. "Speculations on Cosmogony." *Science* **124** (1956):218.

Gribbin, John. "New Thoughts on Space Time." *New Scientist* **42** (1969):11.

———. "New Thoughts on Gravitation." *Cambridge Research* **6** (1970):11.

———. "Retarded Cores, Black Holes and Galaxy Formation." *Nature* **252** (1974):445.

———. *Galaxy Formation*. London: Macmillan; New York: Halstead, 1976.

———. "Thiotimoline and Spoonbending: the Tachyonic Link." *Griffith Observer,* **41** April 1977, 17.

———. *Our Changing Planet*. London; Wildwood and Crowell: New York; 1977

———, and Paul Feldman. *Using Gravity to Determine the Nature of Superluminous Astronomical Objects*. Gravity Research Foundation, 1970.

Gursky, H., and R. Ruffini, eds. *Neutron Stars, Black Holes, and Binary X-ray Sources*. Dordrecht: Reidel, 1975.

Bibliography

Hawking, S. W. "Is the Universe Rotating?" *Monthly Notices of the Royal Astronomical Society* **142** (1969):129.

———. *Black Holes Aren't Black.* Gravity Research Foundation, 1971.

———. "Gravitational Radiation from Colliding Black Holes." *Physical Review Letters* **26** (1971):1344.

———. "Black Holes in General Relativity." *Communications in Mathematical Physics* **25** (1972):152.

———. "A Variational Principle for Black Holes." *Communications in Mathematical Physics* **33** (1973):323.

———. "The Anisotropy of the Universe at Large Times." In *Confrontation of Cosmological Theories with Observations.* Edited by M. S. Longair. Dordrecht: Reidel, 1974.

———. "Black Hole Explosions?" *Nature* **248** (1974):30.

———, and R. K. Sachs. "Causally Continuous Spacetimes." *Communications in Mathematical Physics* **35** (1974):287.

Hills, J. G. "Possible Power Source of Seyfert Galaxies and QSOs." *Nature* **254** (1975):295.

Hjellming, R. M. "Black and White Holes." *Nature Physical Science.* **231** (1971):20.

Holy Bible. King James edition.

Hoyle, Fred. "On the Origin of the Microwave Background." *Astrophysical Journal* **196** (1975):661.

———. *Astronomy and Cosmology.* San Francisco: W. H. Freeman, 1975.

———. *Astronomy Today.* London: Heinemann, 1975; U.S. title: *Highlights in Astronomy.* San Francisco: W. H. Freeman, 1975.

———, and John Elliot. *A for Andromeda.* London: Souvenir Press, 1962; Corgi, 1963.

———, and John Elliot. *The Andromeda Breakthrough.* London: Souvenir, 1964; Corgi, 1966.

———, and Geoffrey Hoyle. *The Inferno.* London: Heinemann, 1973.

————, and J. V. Narlikar. "On the Effects of the Non-Conservation of Baryons in Cosmology." *Proceedings of the Royal Society* **A290** (1966):143.

————. "A Radical Departure from the 'Steady State' Concept in Cosmology." *Proceedings of the Royal Society* **A290** (1966):162.

————. "On the Nature of Mass." *Nature* **233** (1971):41.

————. "Cosmological Models in a Conformally Invariant Gravitational Theory." *Monthly Notices of the Royal Astronomical Society* **155** (1972):323.

Jaakkola, T., K. J. Donner, and P. Teerikerpi. "Two Luminosity Classes of Quasar." *Astrophysics and Space Science* **37** (1975):301.

Jeans, James. *Astronomy and Cosmogony.* London: Cambridge University Press, 1928.

John, Laurie, ed. *Cosmology Now.* London: BBC Publications, 1973.

Jordan, P. *The Expanding Earth.* London: Pergamon, 1971.

Landsberg, P. T., and D. Park. "Entropy in an Oscillating Universe." *Proceedings of the Royal Society* **A346** (1975):485.

Laumer, Keith. *The World Shuffler.* New York: Berkley Publishing, 1970.

Lawrence, J. K., and G. Szamosi. "Statistical Physics, Particle Masses and the Cosmological Coincidences." *Nature* **252** (1974):538.

Layzer, David. "The Arrow of Time." *Scientific American* December 1975, p. 56.

Long, D. R. "Experimental Examination of the Gravitational Inverse Square Law." *Nature* **260** (1976):417.

McCrea, W. H. "Continual Creation." *Monthly Notices of the Royal Astronomical Society* **128** (1964):335.

————. "A Philosophy for Big Bang Cosmology." *Nature* **228** (1970):21.

————. *Halley Lecture,* University of Oxford, 1975. Reported in *Nature* **255** (1975):196. See also *New Scientist* **66** (1975):895.

————. "Ice Ages and the Galaxy." *Nature* **255** (1975): 607.

————. "Solar System as Space Probe." *Observatory* **95** (1975):239.

Meier, David. "Have Primeval Galaxies Been Detected?" *Astrophysical Journal* **203** (1976):L103.

Misner, C. W., K. S. Thorne, and J. A. Wheeler. *Gravitation.* San Francisco: W. H. Freeman, 1973.

Narlikar, J. V. "Steady State Defended," in: *Cosmology Now,* ed. Laurie John. London: BBC Publications, 1973.

————, and K. M. V. Apparao. "White Holes and High Energy Astrophysics." *Astrophysics and Space Science* **35** (1975):321.

————, and E. Sudarshan. "Tachyons and Cosmology." *Monthly Notices of the Royal Astronomical Society* **175** (1976):105.

Nature Physical Science. Special issue on Cygnus X-3. October 23, 1972.

Newton, Isaac. "Letter to Dr. Bentley." Quoted by D. Brewster, *Memoirs of Sir Isaac Newton.* Edinburgh, 1855.

Niven, Larry. *Ringworld.* London: Gollancz, 1970.

————. *Neutron Star.* London: Sphere, 1971.

————. *Protector.* New York: Ballantine, 1973.

————. *Inconstant Moon.* London: Gollancz, 1973.

————. *A Hole in Space.* New York: Ballantine, 1974.

Oster, L. *Modern Astronomy.* New York: Holden-Day, 1973.

Ourassine, L. "Optical Variation of 3C371." *Nature* **254** (1975):125.

Park, David. "Entropy in an Oscillating Universe." *Collective Phenomena* **1** (1973):71.

Pathria, R. K. "The Universe as a Black Hole." *Nature* **240** (1972):298.

Pegg, D. T. "Closed Time and Absorber Theory." *Nature Physical Science* **243** (1973):143.

Penrose, R. "Black Holes," in: *Cosmology Now.* Ed. by Laurie John. London: BBC Publications, 1973.

————, and R. M. Floyd. "Extraction of Rotational Energy from a Black Hole." *Nature Physical Science* **229** (1971): 177.

Phillips, Tom, and Michael Rowan-Robinson. "Molecules Among the Stars." *New Scientist* **69** (1976):170.

Piper, H. Beam. "Gunpowder God." *Analog* LXXIV, November 1964, p. 17.

Pohl, Frederik, and Jack Williamson. *Farthest Star.* London: Pan, 1976.

Press, William, and Saul Teukolsky. "Floating Orbits, Super-radiant Scattering, and the Black-Hole Bomb." *Nature* **238** (1972):211.

Rees, M. J. "Black Holes." *Observatory* **94** (1974):168.

————, R. Ruffini, and J. Wheeler. *Black Holes, Gravitational Waves, and Cosmology.* London: Gordon and Breach, 1974.

————, and W. C. Saslaw. "Massive Black Holes in Extragalactic Source Components?" *Monthly Notices of the Royal Astronomical Society* **171** (1975):53.

Rosen, Joe, and Nathan Rosen. "The Maximum Mass of a Cold Neutron Star." *Astrophysical Journal* **202** (1975): 782.

Ryan, M. P. "Is the Existence of a Galaxy Evidence for a Black Hole at Its Center?" *Astrophysical Journal* **177** (1972):L79.

Sagan, Carl. *The Cosmic Connection.* New York: Doubleday, 1974.

————. *Other Worlds.* New York: Bantam, 1975.

Bibliography

Sandage, A. *The Hubble Atlas of Galaxies*. Washington, D.C.: Carnegie Institution, 1961.

————. "Stars, Galaxies, and the Universe." *Mercury* **3** (1974):18.

Sarfatti, Jack. "Implications of Meta Physics for Psycho-energetic Systems." *Psychoenergetic Systems* **1** (1974).3.

Sciama, D. W. *Modern Cosmology*. London: Cambridge University Press, 1973.

Scientific American. *Frontiers in Astronomy*. San Francisco: W. H. Freeman, 1970.

Sérsic, J. L. "On the Structure of Peculiar Galaxies." *Bulletin of the Astronomical Institutes of Czechoslovakia* **24** (1973):150.

Shakespeare, W. "Hamlet, Prince of Denmark," in, for example: *The Dramatic Works of William Shakespeare*, London: Routledge, 1856.

Shapiro, Stuart, and James Elliot. "Are BL Lac-type Objects Nearby Black Holes?" *Nature* **250** (1974):111.

Shapley, Harlow. *Galaxies*. 3rd ed. Revised by Paul Hodge. Cambridge, Mass.: Harvard University Press, 1973.

Simak, Clifford D. *Ring Around the Sun*. New York: Simon and Schuster, 1953.

Singh, Jagjit. *Modern Cosmology*. Pelican, 1970.

Smith, E. E. "Lensman" series. Published in paperback by Panther, London.

Taylor, John. *Black Holes: The End of the Universe?* London: Souvenir Press, 1973.

————. *Superminds*. London: Macmillan, 1975.

————. Interview. In *BBC Science Magazine,* no. 52, December, 1975.

Terrell, J. "Radio Galaxies and Local QSOs." *Nature* **258** (1975):132.

Tipler, F. J. "Direct-Action Electrodynamics and Magnetic Monopoles." *Il Nuovo Cimento* **28B** (1975):446

Tryon, Edward P. "Is the Universe a Vacuum Fluctuation?" *Nature* **246** (1973):396.

Van Flandern, T. C. "A Determination of the Rate of Change of *G*." *Monthly Notices of the Royal Astronomical Society* **170** (1975):333.

————. "Is Gravity Getting Weaker?" *Scientific American* **234** (1976):44.

Varshni, V. P. "Alternative Explanation for the Spectral Lines Observed in Quasars." *Astrophysics and Space Science* **37** (1975):L1.

Wheeler, John A., ed. *Geometrodynamics*. London: Academic Press, 1962.

Wolfe, A. M., and G. R. Burbidge. "Black Holes in Elliptical Galaxies." *Astrophysical Journal* **161** (1970):419.

INDEX